THE
OPEN
PRISON

SOL CHANELES

THE
OPEN
PRISON

Saving Their Lives and Our Money

THE DIAL PRESS   NEW YORK   1973

Library of Congress Cataloging in Publication Data
Chaneles, Sol.
The open prison.
1. Prisons—United States.   2.   Open prisons—United
States.   I.   Title.
HV9469.C5   365'.973   72–11537

Printed in the United States of America
First Printing
Book design by Margaret McCutcheon Wagner

To
M. L. Volski,
my teacher,
and Janine,
my friend

CONTENTS

INTRODUCTION: REFORM FOR PRISONS OR PRISONERS?

An establishment charged with the responsibility of enforcing the law and given the power to use necessary force and lethal weapons to achieve this purpose should not be entrusted with the task of reforming people who have violated the law. Since the only socially acceptable method at present for punishing offenders, apart from the death penalty, is deprivation of liberty, it is illogical for those whose authority is backed up by guns to be appointed moral instructors. If the purpose of prisons were simply to coerce inmates into accepting and adjusting to prison life, armed keepers would be well suited to the task.

There is almost universal agreement that the purpose of prison is rehabilitation. But rehabilitation programs have not worked and they don't work because they are controlled by law-enforcement agencies—society's instruments for coercion, repression, and punishment.

The primary responsibility for prisoner rehabilitation should be borne by communities outside the sphere of influence of law-enforcement agencies. Since crimes are committed in communities, since prisoners return to communities, the burden of rehabilitation must rest with communities themselves and not with specialized organizations of the state. Communities can, should, and eventually will assume such responsibility.

What would be the advantages in community control of prisoner rehabilitation? Foremost is that preparation for return to a community would be based on actual living conditions, socially realistic attitudes, choices, and opportunities rather than the programmed routine of the insulated prison environment. Prisons in remote rural areas staffed primarily by personnel recruited locally are hardly in a position to equip urban offenders to return to an urban way of life. By bringing prisoners closer to communities—any communities—they can be helped from the very beginning of their sentence to realize that the community is not an antagonist but the basic and inevitable framework in which he has both a major stake and a range of opportunities for voluntarily achieving his aspirations. Almost unlimited choices of meaningful work could be developed in connection with improving communities, for there is no end to the number of ways a community might be improved.

Community responsibility for prisons and prisoner rehabilitation would serve to maintain vital intellectual, social, and emotional ties—lifelines that are cut off under present prison arrangements, needing years to repair after lengthy removal from society.

Closing the gap between prison and community would reduce the staggering costs of perpetuating a system that is nothing less than a colossal failure. Ten million people went through this awful system from 1930 to 1970 at a cost of thirty billion dollars. Between 1970 and 1980 another ten million people will go through the system: an additional thirty billion dollars. Our prisons are the most gilded cages ever conceived, and we have nothing to show except more crime, more hardship on criminal and victim alike, and increased burdens on the community.

The financial savings from effective prisoner *rehabilitation* are likely to be substantial. But this type of dollar benefit to the public is a long way off. What would produce immediate savings would be community responsibility for prisons. Under the assumption that prisoners can be trusted with freedom, many inmates would be released by day, overnight, or on weekends to participate in the life of the community, drastically reducing the number of guards needed; prisoners could be employed part or full time, and thereby pay all or a portion of room and board costs; prison factories could produce goods needed by the communities, such as hospital beds, communications equipment, prosthetic devices for the handicapped, and school furniture.

The current operating costs for keeping one man in prison for one year are close to $15,000. If the capital costs—for land and buildings—were added to operating expenses, the annual bill to the taxpayer for keeping one man locked up would come close to $30,000. Taking the responsibility for prisons away from law-enforcement agencies and vesting it in communities would result in cutting back costs for operations and capital by at least $10,000 per prisoner the first year. An additional savings of 50 per cent would result over the next four to five years.

When the cost of public services is skyrocketing, it pays to get rid of inefficient services. Elementary prison reforms can do much to reduce costs and reduce crime at the same time. For each day that a person is kept in prison as it is presently organized, the future costs to the taxpayer go up: the increased risks of more serious crime, the costs of dependency for the offender and his family, the costs to the victim, the costs of continued disturbances and riots, and the intangible cost of gradual erosion of respect for human life.

At present, prison officials ask for and get more money from the public than ever before, and they get it with little or no explanation to the public about what it is really getting for its money. Operating budgets for prisons double every ten years without any accounting for what has been achieved. If private businesses were run this way they would quickly close down or be destroyed for milking the public so ruthlessly.

Prisoners have expressed a political concern for their situation, as indeed they should, for they too will eventually have to share the burden for these extraordinarily wasteful expenditures. Each day that a man spends in prison represents a lien against his future earnings; the senseless extravagance that surrounds him is surely a disincentive to work. If prisoners could vote on prison budgets, they would cut, cut, cut.

The public is inclined to accept the rhetoric of prison officials in the same way that, until recently, inmates accepted their orders. Prison riots, arson, vandalism, and violence stimulate no major changes either in cost-saving measures or in rehabilitation. What often happens in the aftermath of rioting is that costs go up and rehabilitation efforts are cut back. The prison establishment operates in an air-tight system based on denial of the public's freedom to control its dollars and on the denial of the inmate's freedom to control his future.

The burden of prison failures does not fall on abstract governments, states, or publics. It falls on real people in real communities—communities which produce criminals and which must take back ex-prisoners. The ultimate responsibility for prisons must be the community.

Community responsibility for prisons and prisoners, carried out in a way that assures human integrity and provides opportunities for the exercise of freedom, will help offenders mature more rapidly. This responsibility will also provide communities with a more discerning consciousness and concern for those very shortcomings among free men that lead to trouble with the law in the first place. When we assure the dignity and freedom of others we become the beneficiaries of greater dignity and freedom for ourselves.

THE
OPEN
PRISON

I

THE
EXPLOSIONS
WITHIN

Prisons Need Restructuring
A SEASON OF RIOTS

In 1952, prison riots, like a contagious epidemic, swept across the entire country, visiting terror and destruction on many state and federal prisons. These were not the first . . . or the last. Eighteen years later, beginning in early 1970, a fresh wave of prison riots rocked the nation. The news media, acting under a voluntary code requiring toning down or burying stories about riots (resulting from the urban riots of 1967–68) began telling the public about prison disturbances only after New York City's infamous Tombs had been taken over by prisoners in August 1971. The stories described a familiar pattern of arson, vandalism, defiance, the seizing of guards as hostages, injury and damage to property. A new contagion spread to places that had previously been free of disruption, like juvenile centers and disciplinary barracks for members of the armed services serving sentences for violations of the military codes.

The most tragic and costly prison riot of the twentieth century erupted in New York State's Attica prison. On September 13, 1971, after National Guardsmen, state police, and prison guards restored order, the toll in life was forty-five dead —eleven hostages and thirty-four prisoners. More than a hundred and fifty were wounded, many critically. Immediately after the Attica massacre the contagion spread: Vermont prisoners went on a month-long strike; more than a dozen prisoners were seriously wounded in a riot at the Pontiac, Illinois State Penitentiary and, on October 26, some one hundred rioting U.S. Army offenders, many of them decorated veterans from the senseless slaughter in Southeast Asia, burned down the Army disciplinary barracks in Fort Gordon, Georgia.

The 1970–71 prison riots lasted longer, were more violent and more difficult to quell than prison riots of the past. Prison authorities were startled by an inspired militancy among the inmates. Unlike past demonstrations, the protesting inmates of these were not complaining about prison food, living conditions, or idleness. Heading the long lists of grievances were fundamental issues usually raised by legalists or reformers: Are prisoners entitled to the rights of citizens which are not specifically denied by law? May a prisoner be subject to such punishment as isolation and short rations without due process? May a prisoner be deprived of earned days of "good time" that shorten his sentence without benefit of counsel or appeal? Does censorship of inmate mail constitute a violation of basic constitutional rights? May an inmate be denied the right to worship in the religion of his choice?

The prevailing attitude among sentencing judges, prosecutors, government officials, and prison administrators is that the ends of criminal justice are fully served by a fair trial and a prison sentence. Their view is, once a convicted criminal—man, woman or child—is locked up in a remote prison whose location is unknown to the average person, one need concern himself no further about justice. That a prisoner is also a citizen is a fact which is just beginning to arouse the conscience of America.

In spite of two hundred years of rhetoric about rehabilitation, the person who is convicted of a crime and sentenced to prison merely serves time with little benefit to himself, the community, or the ends of justice. The sentence imposed by judges usually does little more than describe how much time a person must spend behind bars. There are no instructions to prison authorities as to how the *purpose* of the sentence is to be accomplished. Should an illiterate be made literate? Should an unskilled worker be taught a useful occupation? Should a mentally sick prisoner be healed? Should an immature person be educated to wisdom? How are these objectives to be accomplished and by whom? There are no laws designed for the *specifics* of rehabilitation.

In some states judges sentence people to prison for an indeterminate term of one to three years "to be rehabilitated there." This ill-conceived practice has led to the comical but sad situation of prisoners sending hand-written legal briefs to judges trying to prove that they are not rehabilitable and are therefore required to serve no more than the minimum sentence. In the absence of instructions by judges as to what should take place in prison, many prisoners have argued that most forms of imprisonment constitute unconstitutionally cruel and inhuman punishment. They are probably right.

WHAT ARE PRISONS SUPPOSED TO DO?

With no clear formulation of what prisons are supposed to accomplish, coupled with the general indifference of judges and government officials over what happens after a sentence is imposed, it is no wonder that prison officials run prisons as private satrapies. They are rarely accountable to anyone. Except during disturbances, sit-down strikes, and riots, the public rarely has occasion to know who runs the prisons or what prison personnel are supposed to be doing. In the typical press conference during a riot the Commissioner of Correction will say that order is being restored, that he has been well aware of the underlying problems for some time, and that he could do a better job of rehabilitation if the public spent more money for more guards and more prisons. This familiar performance is little more than a snow job. Without explicit legal authority to do more than keep people locked up, without clear instructions regarding the objectives of a sentence, without a specific warning that the rights of prisoners may not be denied without due process, prison officials will do only the minimum to avoid controversy, prevent escapes, and keep the lid on. Doing the minimum just hasn't worked.

The separate world of the prison in which officials carry out policies of systematic deprivation and abuse with impunity has begun to crack. Abused inmates have found that their voices carry across the distance that once gave prisons protective isolation.

The abuses that take place in prison are designed to achieve one objective: to extinguish the inmate's will to be a free man. Monotonous routine, beatings, military lock-step marching, silence, demeaning work, lack of privacy in performing bodily functions, digging mass graves for paupers, obedience to arbitrary rules and punishments, homosexual attacks with apparent tolerance of officials, humiliating taunts, and murder are among the most common abuses. These violent, inhuman actions are not the products of depraved guards and officials. Irrationality, violence, and cruelty probably do not occur more frequently among prison personnel than in the general population.

Prison abuses are not the results either of accident or lapses in management. These acts are part and parcel of a system that fears the longing of men in captivity, that fears the yearnings of men for equality under the law even while they are committed to prison. The only way that prison officials can deal with the potential exercise of undefined prisoner rights is to suppress all rights except those that can be made subject to rigid control. What follows is an environment and routine of behavior that is programmed to the last degrading detail.

So powerful is the prison establishment's need to coercively control an offender's behavior that the same mindless, arbitrary rules are applied to parole conditions. When an offender is released on parole he may not, for instance, marry without official approval, have sexual relations with a woman who is not his wife, consume alcoholic beverages, travel or change jobs without permission. All these restrictions, on top of a prison record, act as a formidable barrier to getting a job and finding a decent place to live. He lives constantly with the knowlege that he is a police suspect.

Demand for obedience and dependence on authority are the hallmarks of prison routine. The rules apply with equal force to eight-year-old chronic truants from school and armed bank robbers, to matronly shoplifters and skid-row alcoholics, many of whom are "senior citizens," to prostitutes as well as professional killers. The effects of these demands are to dull any motivation or interest in using the days and months of imprisonment productively. Chances for learning or self-improvement in the prison environment are very remote and difficult. Most inmates give up.

Education and training programs cannot work in an environment devoted to the repression of thought and the extinction of will. Even the most far-sighted, innovative, and practical programs for education and training are futile if they are not underpinned by a commitment to the belief that, except for the limitations of certain liberties during their sentences, prisoners are free men.

A HUNDRED YEARS OF
DISCIPLINED IDLENESS

In 1970 the members of the American Correctional Association (formerly the American Prison Association) assembled in Cincinnati to celebrate their hundredth anniversary. Following a lengthy pageant in which officials wore the musty uniforms of prison guards used a century ago, the members affirmed their 1870 Declaration of Principle, asserting: "Steady, active, honorable labor, with reasonable compensation to the prisoners, is the basis of all reformatory discipline. It not only aids reformation but is essential to it."

A hundred years have gone by and yet enforced idleness of prisoners remains characteristic of most prisons. Fewer than fifteen out of a hundred inmates receive any kind of compensation for work performed, and the rate of compensation is between five and thirty-five cents an hour—unchanged for the last fifty years.

The absence of meaningful labor and reasonable compensation is really a less troublesome issue than the fact that nearly all prison work programs provide slight opportunity to learn a useful skill or are jobs which exist only in prisons. To provide opportunities would be an invitation to widen the cracks in the separate world of the prison. Prison personnel resent the introduction of modern education, vocational training, and industrial programs. These represent encroachments by the outside world, an invasion of the serene privacy that prisons have enjoyed for nearly two hundred years.

Innovation implies that inmates might get jobs which offer higher pay and greater job satisfaction than the stultifying, suffocating routine of prison work offers to its workers. If prison personnel could change jobs easily without loss of seniority and other benefits, they would not see the enlargement of prisoner's rights as a direct, imminent threat. Eventually, most inmates are released from the system, but prison personnel are not. There are many ways in which personnel suffer more from being trapped by the establishment than do the inmates. All the more reason, as they see it, for keeping things as they are. For this reason, one of the first acts of the prison establishment in the aftermath of a riot is to increase the pay of uniformed guards. For this reason, disciplinary actions are taken against guards who express sympathy for prisoner grievances. Changing the conditions that lead to riots must await dull commission reports that few people read and that are soon forgotten. Token improvements, new and glamorous programs, will bring very little change. Before new programs can show any beneficial results, the prison establishment itself must be reformed. Reform must start with a new definition of the basic issues.

POLITICIZED PRISONERS

The underlying problem of prisoners is political. Most property crimes—robbery, representing about 80 per cent of all crimes committed in the nation—are committed by people who do not have the legal means to get what they need or want. They are poor. They lack education and marketable job skills. The power centers of American society, like the profit centers of business, are carefully protected and guarded. Relatively few people, even with the vote, can participate in decisions which affect distribution of the country's power and affluence. A host of techniques—the sheer deadweight of bureaucratic government, the repressive measures of law-enforcement agencies, and pressures which insist on conformity—are used to stifle public longings for participation.

In prison, every weakness known to American communities

is intensified and magnified. Even simple, everyday needs of inmates can be satisfied in prison only by the use of illegal methods. When public figures describe prisons as "schools for advanced crime," they are aptly defining an environment that offers no choice, no alternative. Access to power, meaningful choices, and the ability to decide on a voluntary basis are at the core of political rights. Until prison reforms are introduced that respond to and assure these rights, prison operations will continue to be an extravagant, two-billion-dollar-a-year waste.

The inmates of the 1970s are younger and better educated than at any time in the past. In addition, they have learned the militant, politically charged language of the massive urban riots that wracked the nation during the late sixties. About 50 per cent of the older men and almost 70 per cent of the younger ones who were arrested and jailed during the urban riots had previous prison records.

Many have gone back to jail for a variety of new crimes. Among the new breed of prisoners are criminals who demonstrate in behalf of disadvantaged minorities, youngsters who have rallied against the sacred cows of the college establishment, and "peace" criminals who are proudly haled off to prison for burning draft cards and resisting the government's war policies.

All the coercive, repressive techniques known to prison officialdom cannot prevent the average inmate from seeing, hearing, and understanding what is going on. Prisoners are beginning to tell themselves to do something about their rights as prisoners. For if they don't do it for themselves, there is no one within or without the prison establishment willing to do it for them. Prisoners have seen, heard, and understood enough; the problem is getting the message to their keepers.

Grievances presented to penal authorities during and following the tragic riots of 1970 and 1971 were a lengthy recital of complex political issues that government and the public have ignored for too long: arbitrary and unfair bail procedures; officially condoned brutality and murder; arbitrary punishment; interminable delays in hearings, trials, and appeals; inadequacy of legal counsel (juveniles in most states receive no legal counsel at all); unfair sentencing practices; unreasonable parole conditions; and idleness. The lists went on and on. How can a man reform in an environment that fosters sexual perversity? How can a man practice reason and communication in a setting in which arbitrariness and brutality are the rule rather than the exception? How can a man respect democratic government without even rudimentary opportunities for participating in self-government? How can mopping and re-mopping a section of corridor to keep busy convey respect or stimulate motivation for a job? How can a man acquire skills for a return to civilian life in an environment that has all the disadvantages of a military organization and none of its highly touted benefits? These were the issues and questions raised.

Accused and convicted criminals became united in protest. Unity among society's lowest element and in behalf of democratic ideals? Hard to believe. One has to go back to the times of slave revolts for comparison. It doesn't often happen that a powerless and humiliated minority stands up to the armed, overwhelming force of its master. When events of this magnitude and quality occur the public must listen.

Prison riots are not capricious, isolated events—they are all infused with a single, controlling impetus: the right to serve a prison sentence in strict accordance with the law. This means compliance with specific legal deprivations *plus* the many protections and guarantees spelled out or implied by law. This single principle has been the one that has motivated much of American history; it is the single idea that will determine much of America's future.

ARE PRISONS NECESSARY?

Do we need prisons at all? Discussions about prisons often gravitate to extremes. On one side are arguments that they are not necessary. On the other it is stated that rehabilitation efforts are a waste of taxpayers' money and that, indeed, we need more and tougher prisons.

Congress and state legislatures reflect vacillation between these extremes. There have been, since 1964, numerous laws proposed that would help maintain an offender's ties with his family by keeping him in his community under conditions of restricted liberty, providing the means for getting an education, skills, a job, and the economic stability believed necessary to prevent further trouble. There are just as many laws proposed that would spend additional billions of dollars to tear down old prisons and build new ones. In March 1971, President Nixon received a standing ovation from a conference of judges when he urged more punishment for offenders.

People who contend that prisons are unnecessary point to inequities in the capitalist system that become explosively exaggerated in the prison environment. Advocates for more and "better" prisons hold up the statistics on increasing crime and the high rates of recidivism as the main rationale for longer sentences, a more punitive approach and more prisons.

Both views represent extremes. The meager grains of truth in each are not sufficient to justify policies based on either. We are going to need prisons for some time to come—in spite of the fact that in the short run prisons do much harm, and in the long run are irrelevant. Neither view touches on one of the main reasons of what is really wrong with prisons: the coercive, programmed life demanded of prisoners that stifles rather than invigorates a sense of self-worth and snuffs out the love of freedom.

WHAT IS REHABILITATION?

Over the past forty years more than ten million Americans have served time in prisons. Most are now lawabiding. They have become our next-door neighbors. They have survived— they have adjusted. The first five years after release from a prison term are the most grueling; it is during this period that the greatest rate of return to prison occurs. Personal anger, humiliation, immaturity, and lack of skills combine with public indifference and the lack of community services make these first years of self-renewal lonely ones piled high with hardship.

But the ex-offenders adjust, and their adjustment has little to do with any prison program of rehabilitation. Some make it just by sheer luck. Many ex-prisoners talk about the "one lucky break" or the patient mother, brother, sweetheart, or wife who made the difference. Others mature out of crime.

Research on offenders concentrates on repeaters; there is virtually no research on ex-prisoners who succeed. That most of the ten million achieve a stable existence is powerful argument that there are things about society in the United States that are good, that there are processes that help, that there are values and opportunities that liberate.

For most Americans becoming "mature" means becoming relatively free of coercive, programmed demands. These demands fall more heavily and unremittingly on the young. America's youth are generally kept in check by unreasonable demands and rules inflexibly enforced by the constant threat of punishment, rules that are set by older people who are free from such restraints. The attitude of the older generation toward prisoners closely resembles their attitude toward the young.

Prisons offer no choice, few satisfactions, and forced predictability rather than stability. Steel bars define not only physical space but also a mental and emotional cage. Basic reformation of the human being cannot take place in a cage. Rehabilitation means a restoration of personal dignity, a building up of purpose and skill, an awareness of one's freedoms and how to exercise them voluntarily and constructively. At present, those released prisoners who do rehabilitate themselves do so only after overcoming debilitative and destructive failures.

Agencies responsible for rehabilitation are actually law-enforcement organizations. In addition to their burden of catching and prosecuting criminals while trying to adhere to standards of justice, they are obliged to provide "helping" services to the very people they seek to punish. Sheriffs who

run county jails and prison farms, wardens who run big penitentiaries, openly scoff at this legally mandated burden for
rehabilitating prisoners. In their view the responsibility boils
down to feeding, preventing escapes, and avoiding mayhem.
But their view is no longer—if it ever was—adequate.

But Will Reform Be?
CITIZENS' CONTROL

Only vocal citizens—with specific powers—are going to be
able to influence the thinking of government executives. As
a beginning, every prison, every probation unit, *every* compo-
nent of the prison establishment ought to have an official
board (not an "advisory" board) of civilians to set prison
policies consistent with laws and emerging court decisions.
They should supervise the implementation of these policies.
They should also seek changes in the laws and seek more
widespread application of judicial decisions.

With the sole exception of President Nixon, no elected
government official has ever taken a strong interest in what
goes on in prison—because nine out of ten prisoners have
never voted, don't vote while imprisoned, and do not yet
actively seek restoration of their voting rights after prison. If
only one out of three of the men and women who were
behind prison walls on Election Day, 1968, had been given
a chance to vote, the outcome of the presidential election
might have been very different.

Until politicians and elected officials become interested in
the private world of the prison, there is an urgent need to

buffer the official and systematic oppression of the prison establishment by interposing citizen boards. The members of these boards should have no affiliation with steel and construction lobbies or the other elements of the "invisible" prison establishment. The members of these boards should be appointed by panels made up of the judiciary, minority group leaders, the news media, and the universities.

It is conceivable that these citizen boards might define part of their task as serving to advocate prisoner rights, or as ombudsmen identifying and responding to grievances. It is desirable that it should happen. But the prospects are dim— that is, if history and tradition are any measures of what is likely to happen.

TWO HUNDRED YEARS OF MINOR REFORMS

The past two hundred years have had no lack of fervent humanitarians pleading on behalf of wretched prisoners in the name of Christian idealism. John Howard, late eighteenth-century penal reformer, was so revolted by the conditions he found in the workhouses and prisons throughout Europe that he advocated the construction of "penitentiaries" where convicts could truly be penitent. With the active support of the Quakers, Howard's compassion for suffering prisoners led to two centuries of uninterrupted prison construction.

Such nineteenth-century prison administrators as Enoch Wines and Zebulon Brockway declared in the late 1860s that penitentiaries were not reforming prisoners, and that what was really needed were "reformatories" in which prisoners could learn a trade and work. They won widespread citizen support; the age of the reformatory began in 1876 in Elmira, New York, heralding nearly a century of unrelenting, unpaid peonage.

There were others, like Dorothea Dix and William Mott Osborne, who roused considerable public support for minimum health standards in prisons, at the same time successfully advocating more rigid discipline among prisoners.

Prison reformers have sought, not an end to prisons, but gradual improvements in the physical conditions there. They urged that inmates should work, not because labor was a way to dignify man, but because it was a way to avoid idleness. These reformers sought to improve sanitary conditions, not because the states' deprivation of the means for a human being to perform elementary bodily functions is demeaning, but because prison corridors smelled bad and offended the sensibilities of visitors performing missions of charity and goodwill.

Their urgings brought about few, inconsequential changes. Most prisons now have modern toilet facilities but inmates have no privacy in using them. (Until 1970, New Haven prisoners, under the jurisdiction of Connecticut's prison Commissioner Ellis C. MacDougall, considered by most of his fellow prison chiefs as the most able and reform-minded member of the establishment, still used wooden bucket toilets under the watchful scrutiny of their keepers.) Most prisons require inmates to work, but under conditions which would be criminally prosecuted were they found in private companies.

Humanitarian prison reform only enhanced the power of prison officialdom, lending public support to traditional concepts and practices. The only genuine prison reform of the nineteenth century came about with the closing in the 1830s of the debtors' prisons. Prison reformers didn't achieve this notable victory; the change resulted from the outrage of underpaid workingmen and women who could no longer tolerate either prison or the poorhouse as inexorable punishment for their inability to get better wages. Debtors' prisons were closed by outrage backed up by bloody strikes, armed clashes with the police, and massive public demonstrations.

The humanitarian approach to improving prisons is still carried on on behalf of prisoners, but is really only a way of sprucing up the prisons and making them look a little better. Contrary to prisoners' complaints, most prisons are clean, compulsively clean. Inmates wash floors over and over each day. While there are occasional signs of vermin and rodents, this is not a general condition. Inmates sleep on beds, often with a soft spring in lieu of mattresses, have blankets but no pillows, and are usually able to keep themselves clean. There is no litter in sight on prison grounds (even cigarette butts are hard to find); where there are lawns or gardens, they are meticulously trimmed and neat-looking. Flogging of inmates has virtually disappeared as a disciplinary practice, but prisoners are still beaten, a practice that officials rigorously deny.

The quality and abundance of prison food—meager and inferior in days gone by when prison officials were given lump-sum budgets for food and could siphon off a tidy profit by cutting down on rations and buying spoiled products—have improved. Many prisons benefit from inexpensive but abundant and nutritious government surplus food. When inmates complain about food it is generally because of monotony rather than because of poor quality.

Many of the physical improvements in prisons have not come about through humanitarian-reformer activity at all. Especially since the end of World War II, the profit-making centers of the nation have pressed successfully to appropriate public funds for unprecedented construction of public buildings. Since 1960 billions of dollars have been spent on the construction and modernization of hospitals, schools, colleges, and other government buildings. Prisons have gotten a portion of these funds, for new buildings, for new equipment. In 1971 there were many bills before Congress to obligate new billions for more public buildings including, on a broader scale than ever before, day-care centers and prisons. Congress seems intent on committing vast sums for prison construction: the Democrats would like to see them built in cities, the Republicans in rural areas. Whenever they are built, dollars will be siphoned off in bribes, graft, and contributions to the political parties' treasuries.

Physical improvements will be made in prisons because new equipment is more costly and profitable than old, because new construction technologies and materials are more profitable than the old. Behind-the-scenes lobbyists for prison construction are not interested in reform. Business seeks profit through construction and sales. The labor unions want to see their members employed. Business and labor are united in promoting massive prison construction.

This kind of unity serves only to perpetuate the failures of the prison establishment. And, unfortunately, citizen boards concerned with setting and overseeing prison policies are more likely to support the unity of business and labor than to address themselves to the problems of prisons and prisoners.

WORK RELEASE — A STEP IN THE RIGHT DIRECTION

In the short run and over time, business, labor, the American public, and prisoners will derive far more benefit from providing jobs to prisoners than through building prisons anywhere. And this is precisely what some enlightened business and labor leaders have been doing, on a very small scale, for the past ten years. Their activity represents a modest kind of prison reform; the practice is called "work release."

The first type of work release for prisoners began in England during the seventeenth century. Prisoners kept aboard a prison brig anchored in the Thames were brought ashore to build and maintain the London docks and waterfront. Only token wages were paid. Contemporary observers of this system of forced labor reported that prisoners learned nothing of enduring value, got no jobs after their prison terms were up, and soon returned to crime and prison.

Modern work release in America operates in about the same way, but most of the jobs are in private business and industry. The worst assignments are janitorial jobs, but there are growing opportunities for work in manufacturing plants and retail establishments. Under some conditions of work release, prisoners are allowed to leave prison from early morning until night, with or without supervision of guards, to work, look for work, visit with family and friends, and take part in sports and public entertainment. But work release of all kinds reached, in 1971, less than one per cent of the prison population.

Effort to relate prisoners to the labor market, especially when it openly and actively involves business, labor, and the public, is beyond criticism. This effort is needed, and deserves far more public attention and support than it has been getting. With appropriate restraint on the freedom of inmates, work release is beneficial in allowing and encouraging a normal, adult style of life. But no matter how broadly this and related programs are expanded, their impact will be negligible, benefiting only a few prisoners—probably the very ones who could do for themselves what costly manpower programs are trying to accomplish for them.

Many of the concerns of prisoners overlap or are identical with those that face millions of other Americans. The difficulties of older prisoners are the same that the older worker must face. The problems of the handicapped prisoner are substantially the same that confront handicapped workers or job-seekers. The problems of the young prisoner between the ages of fifteen and twenty-six, representing almost sixty per cent of our prison population, are essentially those of any American youth with less than a college education, a poor family, or the stigma associated with having the poor judgment to be born into a cultural, religious, ethnic, or racial minority. A prolonged period of high unemployment and the absence of a national commitment to full employment have made the prospects for solving the manpower problems of youth, older workers, handicapped workers and the minorities even more intractable and elusive.

National leaders in periods of high unemployment look upon big public works projects as interim solutions; the public indignation over Attica and a hundred prison riots of 1971 is being molded by public-works lobbyists into a public mandate for more prisons. The average cost for building one prison cell in 1970 was $12,000: it will be $18,000 in 1975. How much better it would be to build jobs instead of cells!

The American public is going to have to face up to the persistent problem of massive unemployment if it is going to do anything about the problems of prisons. Prisoners are going to have to be placed in jobs and trained in them; the prison establishment is the least able of all American institutions to deal with either the narrow problem of prisoner employment or the more complex and critical problem of jobs for young prisoners.

Proposals by the Nixon administration in 1970 and 1971 to decentralize federal manpower authority to municipalities are meritorious; if the proposed legislation included proper safeguards to assure adequate response to the manpower problems of prisoners, much prison reform could be accomplished swiftly and productively. Work-release programs could be expanded to encompass all inmates who want and are able to work; work-release programs under manpower decentralization could match employers' needs to inmates' potentials rather than, as at present, obliging an inmate to take any job available or forfeit the privileges of work release. Under manpower decentralization, many prisoners could enroll in local schools, colleges, and job-training centers, permitting them under minimum restraint to participate actively in the life of their communities.

Other interim arrangements should be encouraged and undertaken. One such arrangement inaugurated in late 1971 is the Brooklyn Businessmen's Committee for the Employment of Offenders. Prominent businessmen have voluntarily undertaken to provide between three and five hundred jobs each year to people to be released from prison—on work release, on parole, or at the end of their sentences—independent of their previous work experience or the nature of their offense. This is the first organized effort in the nation to assert local community responsibility for the employment of prisoners.

The idea was proposed by the author to Frederick W. Richmond, an industrialist and philanthropist who wanted to do something to improve the prison situation. Within an hour, after many telephone calls to Brooklyn's businessmen, Mr. Richmond obtained commitments for hundreds of jobs for prisoners. Within a relatively short time a plan was developed whereby as inmates enter jobs, resources will be made available to them, twenty four hours a day, seven days a week, to help them resolve the many personal and family difficulties they inevitably confront. Funds were sought and found for medical and legal help if needed assistance could not be gotten promptly from public agencies. Employers committed themselves to providing jobs that would lead to more responsibility and promotion rather than the traditional dead-end jobs that are the fate of most prisoners who look for work. Arrangements were made to transfer an offender from one job to another if such a change would lead to more interesting and productive work, greater responsibility, and higher pay. The cost for this effort? Five hundred dollars per offender per year—a figure that should be kept in mind when the prison establishment clamors for more prisons, often forgetting to tell the public that the average cost for keeping one prisoner in prison for a year is $15,000.

The effort on the part of the Brooklyn Businessmen's Committee is only one kind of response as an alternative to the prison establishment. Other efforts could easily be initiated by hospitals assuming responsibility for sick and handicapped prisoners, by schools asserting responsibility for teaching and training young offenders as well as older illiterates, and by citizen groups in general who have grown weary of prison failure.

Prisoners return to local communities. It is there that prison reform must begin.

II

REFORMS, RESTRAINTS, AND RIGHTS

Prisoners and the Law
CLOSE THE PRISONS

America's prisons could be closed without posing any imminent threat to the safety of citizens or to community well-being.

Eventually, the abolishment of all prisons will become a necessity for there is no way to improve upon their present structure, the cost of wasted lives, effort, and financial resources will become oppressively burdensome. All prison reform has but a single goal—the abolishment of prisons.

Present conditions make it possible to initiate a national reform plan that would see the end of prisons within a twelve- to fifteen-year period. With only moderate effort, it is feasible to close down about 6 to 10 per cent of our prisons each year. The reform measures needed to accomplish this include:

- replacing imprisonment by alternatives that will assure the right and obligation of the community to restrain the freedom of those who affront it;

- undertaking, as a matter of high priority, to rehabilitate each year at least 20 per cent of the repeaters in the prison population;

- shifting authority and responsibility for prison management from federal, state, and local governments to local communities;

- creating, under a variety of auspices, behavioral-study and innovative-program centers for those offenders whose criminal careers are marked by violence.

Although police, prosecution, court, and law reforms are necessary and long overdue, it would be a gross mistake to make prison reform contingent on changes in what law-enforcement specialists like to call the criminal-justice system. How criminal laws are enacted and carried out by hundreds of thousands of policemen, prosecutors, judges, and other employees of the criminal-justice system have little effect on prison operations or on the prospects that prisoners face when they reenter communities. When a state like Arizona enacts a law making work release possible for prisoners but does not create the machinery or appropriate the funds to implement work release, no amount of legal, court, or police reform will have any influence in making work release a reality. When a state like New York has a law permitting convicted offenders to pay court-imposed fines on the installment plan in lieu of going to prison but doesn't apply this law, concern with the broader criminal-justice system simply postpones worthwhile and necessary actions.

It will take much longer to institute legal reforms than to reform prisons that have become the dumping grounds for the court's failures. Clearing up the mess of our prisons requires that prison issues be separated from other areas of much-needed reform.

Prison reform requires no new laws, no new money. What it needs is the determined and imaginative application of present laws dealing with prisons and prisoners, and the use of the vast sums, presently being wasted, in ways that will fulfill the mostly forward-looking, practical, sensible intent of the laws.

WHAT IS THE LAW?

Initially, every attorney-general should comb through his state's prison laws to establish, for the first time, a complete inventory of all statutes, and administrative policies relating to prisoners. What will come as a shock to many people as a result of such a survey is not so much that the laws are being applied half-heartedly or cynically but that most of these laws are not being applied at all.

It might come as a shock to some to discover, for example, that although every state makes education mandatory for those up to age sixteen, seventeen, and even in some states eighteen, very few states back up these laws with educational programs for prisoners of mandatory school age. There are notable signs of change. In recent years, Texas has introduced prisoner-education programs that represent a model for reform. Educational districts of the state have been realigned so as to include a prison in each district. Responsibility for prisoner education has shifted away from the prison establishment to politically responsive boards of education. The plan is an exemplary illustration of a reform that not only provides educational resources for prisoners, but, more significantly, changes the political basis for providing fundamental services to the citizens of a state: Texas has broadened the base of citizen concern and responsibility for prisoners. The state has come a long way, for less than forty years ago most Texas prisoners labored, without any form of pay, in chains, under a cruel sun, building roads and highways or harvested cotton crops for private owners, and were disciplined by whipping.

The responsibility for other prison services should be shifted to those who are responsive to social pressures, those who are not immune to criticism. Medical and health services ought to be vested in local districts. Training and work activities, similarly, should be apportioned to local, area-wide, or regional employment and planning councils. No new laws were required for Texas to vest responsibility for prisoner education in educational districts. The appropriate laws were identified and applied with imagination and determination.

The assignment of major prison services to political districts does not preclude, rather it fosters innovative reforms that have been much thought about and tried out in non-prison settings. For example, education and health districts are presently experimenting with the use of vouchers for services. The results are favorable and the plans should be introduced in prisons, not to satisfy humanitarian ideals, but because these experiments provide demonstrated benefits.

PRISONERS AT WORK

When the state's chief law officers look at already existing laws, policies, and procedures relating to the production of prison goods and services they will find that these permit and encourage diverse prison community programs. These laws were formulated in the 1920s and 1930s to correct scandalous abuse and exploitation by businessmen in collusion with prison officials and elected politicians. The laws were also designed to protect organized craft workers from unfair competition by prison labor. Today, neither the unions of craftsmen, industrial, and white-collar workers nor the labor movement in general face any threat from prison labor. Strong unions, the force of public opinion, and increasing enlightenment among prisoners are effective barriers to the exploitation of prison labor by business.

Prison labor represents about 5 per cent of the total American male labor force. There are no laws which prohibit paying these inmates at least minimum wages for their work nor is there any requirement that prisoner labor should be devoted solely to the production of inmate clothing, road signs, and license plates. These laws say that prisoner-made goods and services should be sold and used only in institutions run by government or supported by taxes. Within that framework, it is perfectly legal for prisoners to be gainfully employed in constructing government office buildings, schools, hospitals, and recreation facilities, and not just building of roads. Inmates can be gainfully employed building and maintaining pollution-control equipment, preparing and distributing meals to schools, colleges, and hospitals, instead of making prisoners' shoes and jute sacks.

The expansion of the number and type of production programs that already exist in prisons would represent no revolutionary reform in the present system. Nor would payment of minimum wages necessitate any basic change. Hopefully, it won't be long before prisoners in every type of confinement will receive scale wages for work performed.

Paying wages or making income available to prison inmates might become the basis for real reform if these could reflect a change in the relationship between the state and the inmate worker. If the state employs prisoners, it should follow that inmates are civil servants, as are prison guards, entitled to all the emoluments and benefits accruing to government employees.

It is a truism that a person who works has a responsibility for the quality of the work done and to his employer; the employer has a reciprocal responsibility to the employee. Federal and state laws are continually redefining and regulating employer-employee relationships. But this relationship as it exists between prison establishments and prisoners has been virtually ignored by the American public. Prisons and governments look upon inmate labor as something to be held in contempt and abused rather than as a force to be reckoned with. Present work relationships are based on mistrust and fear that induce inmates to malinger in a minimal form of resistance and guards to intensify force as a means of bypassing employer responsibilities. As employers, prisons should not be exempt from laws governing the responsibilities and conduct of employers. As employees, prisoners should not be

denied the rights and benefits of all working people: the right
to organize and to bargain collectively, the access to grievance
machinery, unemployment insurance, workmen's compensation, social security benefits, and those many other benefits
enjoyed by the free labor force.

People look askance at the prospect of an offender collect-
ing unemployment insurance after getting out of prison if he
is unable to get a job. But if eligibility for unemployment
insurance is based on gainful work during imprisonment, insurance payments to the released offender would represent no
more than the same right enjoyed by most working Americans.

The only control over an offender's life should be an explicit, limited restraint on his freedom until reasonable people
are confident that the potential injury to the community has
been substantially lessened. If government cannot treat prisoner employees on a level of equity with other state employees, then the state should completely surrender its responsibility as employer of prisoners and the responsibility
should be vested elsewhere. Rather than continue the government's exploitive use of prisoners, prisons should be reorgan-
ized as neighborhood or community-owned-and-operated hu-
man-development corporations in which inmates are
employees of concerned neighbors, families, and even former
victims.

But community-owned prisons are just one alternative.
College- and university-run prisons represent another. Private
business operation of prisons is still another choice. The single
most important intermediate objective of prison reform is not

to get government to do more about prisons but to get it to do less and less, eventually getting it entirely out of a business it has carried on with uninterrupted failure for nearly two hundred years.

Tampering with the jobs of members of the prison establishment—who would have to find other jobs—invites criticism of not acting in good faith toward men whose dedication to their jobs entails risk of injury or death. It is precisely "dedication" to prison work that generates conditions endangering life and limb. Dedication to prison employment means carrying out policies that foster hostility, anger, brutality, callousness, and cruelty. Such dedication means working without humane purpose or genuine social benefit. Guards like those at Tucker Prison Farm in Arkansas, who condoned murder and tortured inmates, were praised for their actions by Arkansas Governor Rockefeller as "dedicated." Another Rockefeller, the Governor of New York, when informed that state troopers, police and guards at Attica prison had just completed one of the most tragic massacres in recent American history, praised them as "dedicated."

BARRIERS FOR EX-PRISONERS

When the states' chief legal officers comb the statutes for little-known laws and regulations that prisoners may enjoy as a matter of right, they will find:

- Although there are no laws that prohibit a person with a prison record from moving into a public housing project, administrative policies exist in many states and cities that bar ex-prisoners from decent, low-cost housing.

- Although there are no laws that prohibit ex-prisoners from going to high school, college, or vocational-training centers, most schools bar released offenders from enrollment.

- Although there are only a few laws that prohibit employment of persons who have been convicted to specific types of serious misdemeanors and felonies, most employers (private and governmental) prohibit the employment of nearly all ex-offenders for the first few years after their release from prison.

Illegal barriers to the employment of ex-prisoners are widely known and openly discussed by public and private employers. Although government often exhorts private employers to hire ex-convicts, it has set a notoriously poor example itself by a virtual blanket exclusion of people with prison records. Some progress is being made, however, for ex-offenders are getting token civil-service jobs, but while such tokenism benefits the people who get the jobs, the proportion of those employed to those qualified is infinitesimally small.

In 1970, the United States Department of Labor—which, among all the agencies of the federal government and more than all state and local governments combined, has been mindful of and responsive to the employment dilemmas of the offender—undertook, in cooperation with Georgetown Law School, an important study of the policies and practices of local government in hiring ex-prisoners. The results of the study will fully document the scope of the job obstacles in public employment that faces people with prison records. But is the study really needed? People in the Labor Department know a great deal about illegal employment barriers, and the elaborate study it has undertaken, like most research on government social policies as well as most commission inquiries, is mainly designed to postpone making unpopular or controversial decisions. Research of this kind represents a reprehensible, cynical evasion of the duty to speak out.

A plan of national prison reform requires a simple amendment to civil rights laws, adding nothing new, only clarifying the fact that all job discrimination is prohibited, including barriers to jobs based on previous condition of penal servitude. The issue is not new law, but more rigorous enforcement and application of existing laws, especially those that protect and expand human rights.

Building more abundant and decent housing for all citizens will do more to attack the causes and consequences of criminal actions than construction of prison cells. Improving the scope and quality of education for all Americans, providing access to educational opportunities in communities for prisoners, represents an aspect of prison reform that is far more important than additional education programs in prison. There is less need for costly and unworkable job-training programs in prisons than there is for national policies that create jobs for all Americans who want to work, including jobs for prisoners and released prisoners. There is less need to introduce staff ethnic employment quotas to ease racial tensions in prisons than to take steps to eradicate all racial tension in American life; less need to introduce establishment-controlled quisling inmate councils than to assure all citizens equal access to participation in the affairs of the community.

One reason why prisons don't work is because the prison establishment wants to apply only that narrow spectrum of the law that will preserve and strengthen the establishment's ability to rule. Its power is exercised arbitrarily and with impunity in the face of criticism, protest, and inmate insurrections. The consequences of such power have been two hundred years of cruel and inhuman punishment, repugnant to the consciences of reasonable men and women and prohibited by the Bill of Rights. Increasingly, fair-minded judges will repudiate this illegal exercise of power. Prison reform demands not only that this power should be curbed but that it should be replaced in its entirety.

Prisoners and Society
RISING EXPECTATIONS OR RECEDING RIGHTS?

Many scholars, journalists, elected officials, and spokesmen for national voluntary organizations have recently explained the explosive protests and bloody insurrections of the nineteen-sixties as expressions of the frustration felt by society when its expectations are higher than the nation can deliver. The remedy, according to this view, is to tighten one's belt, expect less, and become more productive. The unprecedented peacetime wage-price controls introduced in 1971 are closely tied to productivity. America's leaders seem to be telling the public that there will be less hardship and more opportunity for those who are more productive.

But the premise that civil unrest and a climate of violence

is a result of unsatisfied and unjustified rising expectations is false. The explanation is nothing less than cynical, political demagoguery. In the two or three years that preceded the tragic riots in Newark and Detroit, interpreters of our national experience were pointing out that the one-third of the nation, ill-clad, ill-housed, and ill-fed, that Franklin D. Roosevelt spoke about in the early nineteen-thirties, had made insignificant progress. Before the massive riots of 1967 and 1968 many people wondered aloud why there was so much poverty in the midst of affluence. The riots, more than five hundred in two years, leaving scores of dead and hundreds of millions of dollars' worth of damage to property, were caused, according to dozens of Presidential Commission studies, by racism, poverty, incompetent local government, by the uncontrolled spread of blight, crime, violence, and by a pervasive sense of powerlessness. The proof was impressive, overwhelming.

The newer explanation, the one preferred by those in power, is calculated to help them preserve their vast power and to be accountable for fewer achievements. The problem is not that people have been promised too much by their leaders or that what has been promised has not been adequately delivered, but that the means for achievement, the means for satisfying old expectations, are kept out of the reach of many people. Access to the means for achievement means access to power; it is a truism that those who possess power are reluctant to part with the least bit of it.

Thus, the cry for law and order has a more general message for America: submit to the discipline of your leaders, pursue the promises of the American Dream—but at a very slow pace; don't expect the remediable injustices that have plagued the nation for a century to be corrected overnight, and don't try to eradicate these injustices at their roots. In short, conform to the rules established by those who have wielded power for generations and don't try to upset the applecart. Behind the cynical message are the major tools for assuring the rule of coercion: wiretapping, bugging, surveillance, accusations of subversion, intimations that outside agitators are at work, and allegations that liberal elements want to turn the country over to welfare recipients and criminals.

The most concentrated version of this line of reasoning and its implications is found in our prisons, but is not unique there.

With occasional lapses into national moods of repression and fear of subversion, the American experiment in democratic government for the benefit of the governed has worked well for almost two hundred years, except for the millions who have been legally and forcefully excluded from the experiment, including our prisoners. The gravest threat to the democratic experiment is the continued exclusion of the powerless from the processes of self-government. The Newark and Detroit riots of 1967 and the Attica and other prison riots of 1971 exemplify what De Tocqueville has referred to as the tyranny of the majority.

There is a compelling need to broaden the scope and opportunities for participatory democracy—without coercion, without the threat of brutalizing discipline. A starting point is rapid reform of American institutions, both those with and those without walls, so that those who are governed genuinely benefit from genuinely representative government. Prison reform must be part of a broad national commitment to minimize and eventually abolish all that is coercive and repressive. Prison management must be transferred from armed agents of establishment repression and violence to the community itself—not because this will lead to better-run prisons but because no free, democratic institutions can survive under the threat of official terror.

WHO'S IN CHARGE HERE?

An important part of the failure of our prisons is due, not to community indifference or ignorance as prison commissioners love to say when appealing for public support, but to the lack of any clear, direct responsibility for what happens in prison.

Local community responsibility for *ex*-prisoners has worked, informally, without laws, without guards, uniforms, or the technology of coercion. Over ten million living Americans have been in prison and have overcome bitter experiences there. They have made it back to civilian life primarily through their own efforts and with informal community support. They have been restored to active and useful lives as free people. The ten million who have been there and back represent massive testimony that opportunity and not force leads the way to cooperation and peacefulness. Prison reform must succeed in gradually dismantling the prison establishment and replacing it with broad community processes that have worked well, generally without constant threat of repression or the use of deadly force.

Vesting communities with responsibility and the money resources for running prisons would open new opportunities for sharing power and create at the same time, incentives for broader public concern for prisoners. It would be vital for Congress to establish national minimum standards providing for the protection of community-run programs against take-over by powerful interests. With adequate safeguards, it would make no difference whether community-run prisons are operated by aerospace corporations or ghetto coopera-tives. One of the more important safeguards would be ac-countability of community-run prison operations to the pub-lic at large rather than to some bureaucratic cog in the machinery of government.

ARBITRATED, NOT ARBITRARY, RESTRAINTS

Prison reform cannot avoid the need to place restraints on the freedoms of those convicted of crime. Some form of restraint is essential if the chances for the commission of new crimes are to be minimized. But such restraint need not be oppressive or demeaning. Restraint need not be carried out by badge-and-gun-toting probation and parole agents who are little more than plainclothes prison guards. A precedent for non-coercive restraint is to be found in arbitration and media-tion mechanisms. These are among the more successful for the reduction and resolution of conflict.

Increasingly, labor disputes, community power clashes, and racial tensions are being cooled or effectively resolved by recourse to impartial arbitration and mediation. It is to such voluntary, free process that we ought to turn for deciding upon the most appropriate form of restraint on the freedom of fellow citizens convicted of crime. Congress can and should promulgate the means and safeguards for such voluntary processes, but the substance of restraint should be negotiated and arrived at by mutual agreement between community residents, representatives of the law, the victim, and the offender himself. Congress should encourage and facilitate a wide variety of arbitration models. Some should be incorporated into on-going labor-management arbitration arrangements, others could be grafted onto community-dispute settlement centers or established in community and neighborhood centers, in schools and intergroup relations organizations.

Arbitration and mediation seek to accomodate the needs of parties in dispute, each willing to give a bit, each getting something so that both are able to go about their lives more cooperatively and peacefully. The offender is a person in dispute with his community. Pulverizing his humanity as we do in prison serves no enduring worthwhile purpose. Imposing reasonable and acceptable restraints on the offender's freedom in a process that assures the offender's participation in determining the restraint, as opposed to our present archaic system that merely requires that we inform him of his legal guilt, is likely to reduce the offender's dispute with his community. Conditions of restraint that would be formulated by arbitration would have to be consistent with opportunities and general restraints that exist for all citizens in local communities. This is why no prison, no matter where it is located, can improve upon its practices: It is an unreal world that does not and cannot correspond to real community life.

By shifting the emphasis of a court sentence from useless and counterproductive coercion and punishment to arbitration and mediation, avenues would open up to reparation, restitution, and restoration designed to bring the offender into community involvement from which he was previously excluded. Prison confinement merely intensifies that exclusion.

The kinds of rights, privileges and freedoms that offenders would have to give up in order to assure the community of appropriate restraint would depend on what a community arbitration board is prepared to accept and what the offender is prepared to live up to.

Giving up the right to vote, even if this right were not automatically taken away by the state upon conviction for certain types of crime, should not enter into consideration as a restraint of a person's freedom. Few of our prisoners, even when they were free men, ever voted. In this respect prisoners resemble the 50 per cent of America's eligible voters who don't vote in local elections or the 40 per cent who don't vote in presidential elections. If the states' legislatures do not restore voting rights to all prisoners, no matter what offenses they have committed, then the Supreme Court should strike down any infringement of the voting right as unconstitutional.

Taking away the right to buy alcoholic beverages and to have sexual relations with a person who is not a spouse are two of the foolish conditions of probation and parole applied in nearly all the states. These are, practically speaking, unenforceable restraints, and they so trespass on a person's privacy as to constitute an intolerable invasion of his integrity. Such trespasses make all other rights abstract, unattainable ideals.

The right to be educated or trained for a job is so fundamental to most of our prisoners who are undereducated and undertrained that placing restraint on this right would be self-defeating for the community. The same is true for restraint placed on any form of legal employment.

Restraint on a person's freedom should be in a form calculated to produce some tangible benefit to both the offender and the community. Performance of a public service for a period of time would be restraint that leads to some benefit. For the offender there is the opportunity to compensate the community in ways that are equivalent to restitution. As part of a national prison-reform plan it would be desirable for Congress to establish local, statewide, regional, and national domestic service corps in which, on a part-time or full-time basis, offenders may contribute to the collective well-being. A domestic service corps need not wait on Congressional will; the President has authority to establish or expand on-going programs by executive order. Prison reform would make a quantum leap were he to do so. For offenders involved in domestic service programs, local community arbitration and mediation groups would, with the participation of offenders, determine whether the terms of their mutual agreements were being fulfilled.

A service corps should not be a vehicle exclusively for offenders to compensate society for wrongs inflicted in a criminal way. This would be little more than still another prison. A service corps more and more is becoming both necessity and opportunity for all Americans to participate directly in the work of making the country a better place to live in. Because it is a device for the enhanced participation for all Americans, it is an appropriate and desirable avenue of participation for offenders.

SAFER STREETS OR FIRMER CONTROLS?

Under the unrelenting prodding of President Lyndon Johnson, Congress passed the Omnibus Crime Control Act of 1968, popularly called the Safe Streets Act. In its potential for bringing about profound reform in police, court, and prison policies and practices, the law represents a major, bold step forward. The law provided a fundamental mandate to do things differently, better; billions of dollars were appropriated providing incentives to state and local governmental agencies to innovate and experiment.

But since its enactment in 1968, billions of dollars have gone down the drain with little to show for either the effort or the money. The Safe Streets Act has enriched manufacturers of tanks for use against American citizens, bullets to kill them and bugging devices to destroy their privacy. Little money has been put into local labor markets to create jobs and the wherewithal for offenders to acquire homes, education, and a pattern of life that cherishes freedom and growth. Vast sums have been spent, under the Safe Streets Act, to train prison guards in methods of riot control, rather than educating them as teachers and agents of social restoration. The Safe Streets Act did not require more bullets than education, or the exclusion of either. The law specifically called for *community-based* prison programs with appropriate safeguards for the representation of community residents, but in 1971 there were fewer community-based programs than there were in 1968 when the law was passed. The politics of the power centers have seen to it that Congressional appropriations were turned into huge profits for such items as prison urinals containing electronic surveillance devices, television monitors providing prison guards with the instruments of Big Brother-·ism, new kitchen and laundry equipment making it easier for prison administrators to exploit inmate labor, and lucrative contracts for building new prisons. Before the enactment of the Safe Streets Act, Congress had passed many laws and appropriated many millions of dollars to encourage new prisoner-rehabilitation programs for juveniles and adults, and there is little to show for these massive expenditures except dusty reports telling about the innumerable interferences preventing achievement of the many possibilities envisioned by Congress.

Congress can but rarely exert pressures on the President and the sprawling, often lethargic, executive branch, to see that its laws are given more than token application. On the other hand, presidents have often, and to good advantage, gone well beyond the limited scope of congressional action. In this regard President Richard M. Nixon has brought about more prison reform than all his predecessors combined. In the first two years of his presidency, Nixon produced more change in the power relationships that dominate prisons than in the nearly two-hundred-year history of American prisons. This amazing achievement could not have been done without the means provided in the Safe Streets Act, passed in the last months of the Johnson administration. But the President could have ignored or given only token attention to the reform possibilities of the Safe Streets Act in much the same way that he has all but turned his back on model-cities and economic-opportunity legislation, also enacted at the urging of his predecessor. Frequently telling the American people and his cabinet members that American prisons represent a spectacular case of uninterrupted failure, President Nixon has gone on to press for reform: broadened use of community-treatment facilities for federal prisoners; federally supported work-release programs carried on in cooperation with state prisons (the number of prisoners on work release in 1970, for example, was greater than the total number who participated in work release from 1930 up to 1970); countenancing the Chief Justice's repeated appeals for prison reform; encouraging community and business groups to become intensively involved in prisoner education, job training, and job placement; insisting, as a condition for granting money to state governments, on greater use of community programs in lieu of imprisonment. In addition, the first three years of his administration, President Nixon created two Presidential Task Forces on the problems of prisons and convened, for the first time in two hundred years, a national conference on these problems. No previous President, no previous Congress— Republican or Democratic—has done so much to stimulate prison reform; but while Nixon's dedication and accomplishment are extraordinary, he has only lighted the first candle at the beginning of a long, dark tunnel.

SOME RESPONSIBILITIES CAN'T BE DELEGATED

In our continuing experiment with democracy, we have given responsibility and authority to agents of local, state, and the federal governments to confine people who have criminally offended, wronged, and hurt us. But we have been excessively vague in telling the agents of our government what to do with and on behalf of these people. We have been both vague and mostly silent in telling offenders what they might be doing on their own behalf. And because we have avoided coming to grips with the most difficult of our domestic problems, we have allowed the authority of prison officials and the establishments they represent to degenerate into brutality, degradation, and mass murder. Until 1969, the federal courts continued to condone the use by Arkansas prison officials of a five-foot whip to lash prisoners for infractions of prison rules. One of the rules that brought about the most lashing was one that forbade prisoners to tell outsiders that mattresses and bedding intended for use by prisoners were being sold by guards. These practices continue in most prisons; correction of these practices will result in less corruption in prison but will not make for better prisons.

Even where prisons are relatively free of corruption, murder of inmates takes place regularly with the knowledge, complicity, and participation of the guards.

The time has come for the American people to recognize that our experiment with prisons as a means for responding to the problems posed by convicted criminals has been an extravagantly wasteful failure. The time has come to abandon the folly of our prisons by embarking on fresh, practical alternatives.

A national program of prison reform requires that we agree on a timetable for the effective restoration of offenders to the community, and a reasonable schedule for the closing of most prisons. A prison-reform commitment also needs the resources to develop and test the effectiveness of remedies for violent behavior, and the concomitant creation of avenues for expressing grievances that will not beget more violence. We will have to convict and confine violent people, muggers, rioting policemen, brutal custodians in all institutions of involuntary confinement, until we understand and develop the measures to help people curb the violence that seethes within them. We will have to confine violent people for as long as it takes for them to mature out of violence.

We cannot entrust the difficult task of helping people achieve maturity to those to whom we give the right to use discretionary force and lethal weapons in a confined environment. To continue to do so will invite only more brutality and violence. The task of restoring lives, teaching and fostering maturity, belongs to the American people in local communities. It does not require specialized agents of coercion or repression. People do not and cannot mature according to any absolute standards. The standards of maturity that have permitted the American democratic experience to flourish, even in the worst times, is a simple, pragmatic one. It involves the maximum freedom, the trust and conviction that we are able to help each other achieve a meaningful life—if not by directly assisting our neighbors then at least by not hindering them from their own purposes.

PRISONS

HOW MANY ARE THERE?

One of the strange things about the prison world is that until 1971 nobody seemed to know or care about how many prisons or prisoners there were in America at any moment. In 1961 when prison officials were asked these questions by Congressional committees, the experts replied that they could only estimate the number of prisons as between twenty-five hundred and four thousand and they couldn't even venture a guess as to how many people were confined.

In February 1971, the Bureau of the Census, carrying out a recommendation of President Nixon's Task Force on Prisoner Rehabilitation calling for an accurate determination, reported that there were 4,037 locally administered prisons for adults. Not included were federal and state prisons, institutions for juveniles, drunk tanks, and police lockups which confine people no more than a few days. There are about four hundred prisons for adults run by the federal and state governments and an additional three hundred establishments for juveniles. On an average day there are about 400,000 people confined in America's prisons: about 161,000 in locally run institutions, 200,000 in prisons run by the state and federal governments, and 39,000 juveniles imprisoned by state and local authorities. But this is only a fragment of a larger picture of prison authority: for every person behind bars awaiting trial or serving a sentence, four convicted persons are under the control of probation and parole agents.

WHAT ARE THEY?

For the past forty years prisons, previously called penitentiaries, have been called correctional institutions, but the changed name reflects no other change. President Nixon, Chief Justice Warren Burger, many governors, hundreds of prison administrators and social scientists, have all said that correctional institutions don't correct. No matter what they are called, places where people are involuntarily kept as prisoners are prisons, no matter what the ostensible purpose, no matter what the local name. A training school for juvenile delinquents is a prison, and so are the workhouses, detention centers, forestry camps, vocational institutions, conservation camps, retrieve units, state schools, work farms, diagnostic facilities, reformatories, country residences, halfway houses, pre-release homes, and community treatment centers. People are sent there as part of a sentence upon conviction of a crime. What happens is essentially the same in each facility.

Halfway houses in the nation's capital are physically more attractive than those in New York City and Chicago, but the discipline is the same, not different from the rules applied in prisons. Federal prisons serve more abundant meals and provide inmates with more regular changes of clothing and bedding than state prisons. Big city prisons like those in Los Angeles and Philadelphia, Hartford and Richmond are kept cleaner, allowing inmates more of a chance to bathe at least once a week than most small city prisons that are rat-and-vermin-infested, using only unsanitary, primitive toilet facilities—eleven per cent of Massachusetts' prisons have no toilet facilities at all.

WHERE ARE THEY?

Except for the handful of prisons located in the largest metropolitan centers of the nation, most of our nearly 4,800 prisons are far removed from cities. The larger ones are situated in the vicinity of small, rural towns, usually with a population of two to three thousand people. Most of the townspeople gave up farming when the land played out, and the men, along with many of their wives, went to work for the prison. These are one-industry towns—the prison is the industry—like Attica in New York, Windsor in Vermont, Chino in California, Lewisburg in Pennsylvania, and Leavenworth in Kansas.

There are many rural prisons in such remote areas that people ten miles away have little awareness of the places and little idea what goes on there, places like Wetampka, Pine

Bluff, Tecachapi, Montville, Occoquam, Henryville, Tillery, and Barazzoris. These are prisons that are truly "a million miles from nowhere." They are located off the main state and county roads. There are no signs pointing in their direction; if people didn't actually work or get sentenced there, it would be hard to believe in their actual existence.

Shortly after Richard Ogilvie was inaugurated as Governor of Illinois in 1969, a newspaper reporter asked him how many prisons and prisoners there were in the state. The governor turned to his prison chief. The prison chief shrugged and turned to an aide, who similarly shrugged in ignorance. Governor Ogilvie promised the newsman an answer—and it took a research project, a hundred thousand dollars, and three months to answer the question. But three years later, under the leadership of the governor and his new prison chief Peter Benzinger, Illinois has undertaken bold, imaginative prison-reform programs that are exemplary in concept and execution.

Illinois is an exception, and it is only beginning to respond to two centuries of ignorance and abuse. It would require an outraged public outcry to find out where our prisons are, precisely how many people are caged in them and what goes on there at taxpayers' expense.

IV

THE
PRISON
ESTABLISHMENT

Punishment

PUNISHMENT AS A WAY OF LIFE

There are about 200,000 people in the United States whose job it is to keep prisoners in confinement or to supervise, with the threat of confinement for any possible infractions, probationers and parolees. The number does not include police, public prosecutors, lawyers, or judges, nor does it include elected legislators or the many governmental agencies that have only minor involvement with prisons and prisoners. These 200,000 people represent the most visible portion of the prison establishment. Their job is to exact a pound of flesh in the name of the American people's desire for retribution: in short, their job is to punish.

Punishment can achieve no useful social purpose. It promotes no benefits to the individual who is punished or to the society that punishes. Punishment that is applied by law is only one end of a spectrum of punishing activity that people carry on against those who, justly and unjustly, become subject to coercive control. Parents punish their children; some with such irrational fury that children are often permanently maimed or killed.

Schoolteachers punish their students, some with such mindless insensitivity that hundreds of thousands of children each year lose interest in schoolwork, accepting their teachers' assessments of them as sluggish, lazy, unmotivated, and incompetent. Is it any wonder that classrooms have become a compulsory hell for so many youngsters? Through their truancy, ungovernability, and acts of delinquency they are expressing a form of resistance to the punishing tyranny of their elders. Close to ten per cent of California's prison population is made up of school truants. Fifteen thousand children, in 1971, were sent to a variety of juvenile prisons in New York State because, although they had committed no offense, they were deemed by the courts as needing supervision, or in danger of becoming delinquent.

DEFENDING THE SOCIAL COMPACT

It is easy to punish. It is hard to remedy the consequences of punishment. Part of the cry for law and order is a reflection of the majority's reluctance to abandon punishment; the cry is also an appeal for more effective ways to preserve and enhance the social compact without resort to methods that undermine and destroy it.

America's main agency for enforcing the social compact by means of punishment is the prison establishment. Penologists and others actively concerned with prisons agree that there has been progress in more humane and productive attitudes in the application of official punishment over the last two hundred years. They point to a shift from the earlier emphasis of making punishment fit the crime to a more recent concept of making punishment fit the criminal. But the difference in emphasis is purely semantic, having little revelance to practice—punishment is still what violators of the social compact are subject to. Reform of penal philosophy and the so-called science of punishment is an ephemeral, fruitless pursuit. Prison practices are the things that require reform and, insofar as these practices are carried out by people whose jobs call for carrying out rules and observing traditions, the rules and traditions need to be changed.

The punitive practices of the prison establishment owe no tribute to Judeo-Christian traditions. Still less is owed to the ideals embedded in the Bill of Rights. The essence of the prison establishment's philosophy is that violation of the law requires the loss of all rights except the right to expiate the crime and to be penitent about the offense. To assure concentrated expiation and penitence, costly fortresses were constructed called penitentiaries and more recently referred to euphemistically as "correctional institutions."

To enforce deprivation of all rights, to assure penitence, the visible prison establishment is little more than an armed military organization—one that is equipped with attack dogs, machine guns, billy sticks, devices to apply electric shock to the genitals, electronic surveillance equipment, vomiting gas and, most recently, depressant and tranquilizing drugs. While Billy Graham and 350,000 persons were celebrating "Honor America Day" in Washington, D.C., a prison riot was starting at Holmesburg Prison in Philadelphia where a national pharmaceutical company was paying prison personnel to experiment on inmates with untested, dangerous drugs, in a manner that reminds one of "experiments" in Dachau. While Labor Day speeches in 1969 were being delivered from the steps of the capitol in Kansas, guards at the state's penitentiary were forcing prisoners to manufacture leather goods without pay and for the private profit of the guards, as similar goods were manufactured by the inmates of the Nazi slave-labor camp at Mathausen. The massacre of forty-five inmates and hostages at Attica, added to the 3,000 inmates who are murdered in American prisons each year, is a phenomenon not much different from official punishment meted out in Babi Yar, Guernica, My Lai, and Auschwitz.

Present-day justification for the existence of the prison establishment derives from the hegemony that state and local governments have assumed over the freedom-restraining, punishing process. A prison is the Frankenstein monster of this hegemony. But before the monster can be transformed, the suzerainty must be abolished. This is the starting point for prison reform. State and local governments cannot be entrusted with so fundamental a responsibility as the restraint of freedom. This is a responsibility for the people at-large. The rapidity with which we are able to shut down unnecessary prisons, and change the character of those institutions that must remain for the time being, will depend on the rapidity with which the American people reclaim the power and rights which are theirs.

Criticism of the prison establishment is not directed solely to the tens of thousands of men and women who have taken vague orders to punish as a broad mandate for inflicting diabolically inventive measures of degradation and torture. Though prison employees are agents for the denial of equal rights under the law, the denial of equal treatment under the law, the denial of equal opportunity under the law, they are not, individually, responsible for maintaining our prisons as peonage camps and crime colleges. The criticism will have to be directed also to state legislators who steadfastly refuse to spell out what should or should not go on in prisons.

The judiciary has also to take criticism. Until 1968, judges refused to prescribe the purposes of a prison sentence and also refused to tell prison administrators that what they were doing was patently illegal. Judges observing the traditional separation of powers between judicial, legislative, and executive agencies, adhered to a hands-off doctrine which required them to refrain from telling prison officials how to perform their work. In 1968, the Supreme Court ruled that states' prisoners could not be denied the protections of the Civil Rights laws merely because they were being kept in involuntary confinement. In court after court judges began reading, for the first time, crudely prepared handwritten petitions from prisoners alleging brutality, denial of habeas corpus, and massive infringements on rights not specifically denied by law. The hands-off policy began to yield, not to prisoner grievances but to a gradual and more vocal assertion that the power of government cannot trample on the rights of its citizens, including prisoners. But a firm direction has not yet been established.

"REFORM" AND THE POUND OF FLESH

Periodic waves of prison "reform" have done little more than introduce administrative changes like separating older from younger offenders, repeaters from first offenders, drunks and vagrants from felons. These waves of reform have centered on the humanitarian need to improve the cleanliness of prisons, upgrade the quality of food, allow for more regular changes of clothing, more frequent family visiting. But these well-intended efforts have avoided the question of punishment entirely, as well as the issue of the aptness of the prison establishment to run prisons. And because the public has been satisfied with humanitarian concessions, the establishment's power has increased and become more arrogant, more indifferent to the small number of outside voices clamoring for change.

What the public should be made aware of is that the prison establishment exacts a heavy price for every concession in the name of humanitarianism. For every new law book made available to prisoners, many guards are sent to specialized schools to learn the use of lethal weapons. For every new shower that is installed, a prison arsenal is created with Mace and tear gas. For every improved inmate meal, guards get increased salaries. In 1969, John Gardner, then Secretary of Health, Education and Welfare, referred to our prisons as "crime factories" and ordered an expenditure of $1.5 million to provide basic literacy instructions for states' prisoners. In that same year, President Richard Nixon said that prisons are "a convincing case of failure." Yet in that year, the states authorized funds for the construction of almost 2,500 new prisons.

The awful price to the public for speciously humanitarian gestures rather than basic prison reform is billions for prison construction with its kickbacks to political parties and the creation of patronage posts.

For inmates, prison is unrelenting hell; for the public it is an extravagant yoke; for the prison establishment, it continues to be a golden goose.

The Punishers
THE ESTABLISHMENTS — VISIBLE AND INVISIBLE

The chief elements that make up the most visible part of the prison establishment are: an agency of government responsible for running prisons usually called a Department of Corrections or Department of Institutions; separate probation and parole departments; a separate agency for running juvenile institutions; also, since 1969, state as well as local planning agencies set up primarily to request and distribute federal funds for various law enforcement activities including prisons; a sheriff's department; and, specialized units of the police, courts, prosecutor's offices whose purpose are to coordinate their respective functions with the prisons. Other visible but less conspicuous parts of the establishment are state and local level legislative committees concerned with prisons as well as special units of state and local government fiscal offices that act on budget requests from prisons. Other components of the establishment are numerous associations that come to the aid of prison officials when they are criticized, testify about their need for more money to do their job, help to whitewash scandals as they erupt, provide employment to establishmentarians on retirement or dismissal from office. These are usually agencies that receive all or a major portion of their operating expenses from government contracts and grants.

The less publicized aspect of the prison establishment is made up of architects who want to design prisons, contractors who want to build them, steel, brick, and mortar companies that want to sell prison merchandise. It is composed of businesses that want to sell food, raw materials, machinery, maintenance services, computers, and handcuffs. The invisible establishment includes companies that manufacture prison surveillance equipment and urinals—many former prison officials are employees of these organizations—and it includes arms manufacturers as well as firms that want to modernize the industrial laundry plants of prisons. It includes real estate operators who promote building new prisons so they can sell land, and pharmaceutical companies so that they can have an uninterrupted supply of human guinea pigs for their drug experiments. Punishment is a highly profitable business in America.

While the foregoing picture represents the prison establishment framework especially on the state and local level, it is an outline, with only minor differences, of the federal prison establishment as well. The most powerful members of the visible prison establishment are not, as one might imagine, the Commissioners or Directors of the governmental agencies responsible for running prison departments and their extensions—probation, parole and other community services —but those who run the smaller parts of the system; the individual prisons, the juvenile institutions, and those who supervise extension services like halfway houses and community treatment facilities.

The most powerful members of the prison establishment are the sheriffs who are most often elected to the post. There are about three thousand of them, nearly one for every county in America, and each sheriff has the responsibility for running a local prison system. Of the nearly 2,000 wardens, principal keepers, and superintendents of local, state and federal prisons of all kinds, nine out of ten have been appointed by governors and prison commissioners acting under pressure and persuasion from many of the components of the prison establishment. Where they have taken competitive civil service examinations for promotion to their high positions, the exams have been rigged so as to favor their candidacy. Nearly all are permanent civil servants; their job security is unassailable. Their job commitment? Preservation of the rules and traditions of a two-hundred-year-old code of punishment. No wall could be built without their approval, no wall torn down without their threat that mayhem would ensue. Most live on or near prison grounds in rent-free homes, furnished by the government down to the last choice steak from the prison kitchen. They live in baronial splendor, attended by unpaid inmate servants, chauffered in government vehicles by prison-er-trustees and plied with handsome gifts and other expressions of esteem by the sales agents of the hidden establishment.

In 1970, the national average salary for the most powerful people in the prison establishment—sheriffs and wardens—was $20,000, about twice the salary of the average college professor and only slightly less than the average college president. Federal prison wardens and wardens of the more populous states earn between $30,000 and $40,000 a year, more than the presidents of many universities, more than executives of corporations employing three to five thousand workers.

The college president is accountable to trustees, faculty, students, parents, alumni, benefactors and the community at large. Only when flare-ups occur, when riots cause the burning down of entire sections of prisons, when the dead and wounded become front-page stories is there a semblance of a prison chief's accountability to someone. For the most part, the main job of the prison chief seems to be to stifle both free inquiry and its expression.

THE TRADITION OF MILITARY DISCIPLINE

More than the people—commissioners, wardens, sheriffs and their nearly 200,000-man cadre—more than the visible and invisible organizations and lobby groups who make up the prison establishment, the establishment is a two-hundred-year-old tradition. The principal pillar of this tradition is the maintenance of discipline among prisoners. Prisons have taken most of their practices, ideals and even dress, from the military—the repository of a religious worship of discipline and punishment for its violation. Among the more articulate spokesmen for this tradition are the American Correctional Association and the Salvation Army. Both cherish military hierarchy and uniforms, both advocate discipline: one because it is considered indispensable for the running of prisons, the other considers it a steppingstone to individual salvation. Both are frequently called upon to vouch for a prison's need for more money.

Although prisons could, and for many prisoners should, be like colleges but not colleges of crime, providing opportunities for intellectual, moral, and social maturation, they are in fact war-game centers for miniature armies of occupation. Commissioners, sheriffs, wardens, and superintendents are the generals—some even wear dress uniforms with gold or silver braid, stars, or other symbols of rank. Subordinates are required to salute. There are colonels, majors, captains, lieutenants, sergeants and, at the lowest rank, guards or officers. Formal communication is not by memorandum but by "orders." Flags fly, drums roll, bugles blare, the cadres march and drill military style carrying rifles and side arms. When, in 1970, New York City's Mayor John Lindsay visited the city's penitentiary on an island in the East River (this is the largest prison in the world, housing nearly 5,000 inmates) for a graduation ceremony of inmates who had completed a vocational training course, he was greeted with a one-hour full-dress military parade of prison staff. In our prisons, inmates are required to march in step to and from prison activities. When they speak back to guards, their action is neither rudeness nor plain sass, but insubordination. The army of occupation rules a conquered, subdued people. The army is prepared to suppress an uprising on the part of the conquered. Guarded prison arsenals contain the weaponry for the task. Federal funds amounting to over ten million dollars were spent in 1969–70 to furnish prisons with armored vehicles, kept not on prison grounds but concealed in nearby camouflaged barns and sheds. Troop reinforcements are available on short notice from the state police, the National Guard, and the U.S. Army. Many inmates, promised shorter sentences or early releases on parole, act as infiltrators and informers to supply intelligence to the prison chiefs.

The basic training of prison staff is strictly in military procedure, including target practice—and when prison guards present demands to their superiors, they include in their request not only higher pay but more paid time off for target practice. All this leaves little or no room for anything other than the pacification of the prisoners. In order to improve their own salaries and working conditions, the military traditions and concepts of uniformed prison staff are energetically supported by other components of the prison establishment, such as the Correctional Education Association, the Correctional Psychologists Association, the Correctional Chaplains Association, the National Association of Training Schools and Juvenile Agencies, and the Prison Industries Association.

THE ESTABLISHMENT: CAN IT BE CONTROLLED?

Civilian leaders, elected and appointed, have as many trepidations over telling prisons' military officialdom what to do as a mayor fears telling his police department what to do, or the President and his civilian cabinet in telling the Pentagon what to do. Military establishments of all kinds usually respond to an attempted intrusion by civilians into their realm by stating that they will not be responsible for the consequences of the suggested behavior. For the Pentagon the fear that is dramatized is an erosion of national security; for the police, a breakdown in morale; for prison guards, possible escapes, disturbances, and riots. The allies of the Pentagon are corporations that depend on contracts to build military equipment, and these are the same allies that support the demands of prison officials for more construction, more armaments, more money. In the worlds of the Pentagon and prisons, civilians are a nuisance; barriers must be erected to keep them away and uninformed if not misinformed. Just as there should be effective civilian control of America's military apparatus, there should be effective civilian control of the prison apparatus.

Dismantling the military organizations of our prisons and replacing them with civilian personnel, along the lines of a college, would remove most of what is irrational and bad about prisons: a tenacious tradition of rigid rules, omnipresent symbols and arrangements of ultimate authority—the discretionary power to kill. The dismantling would also rid prisons of the pervasive sense of being places for the armed occupation of a subjugated population. There is a need for security, but not any more than is required for a large housing project, department store, playground, or factory.

Unless the federal government nationalizes and takes over all prisons, there is no way of trying to deal with America's prisons as a single entity. Each prison army of occupation is relatively autonomous, relating to but not strictly accountable to local vested interests in government and business. There is no monolithic prison establishment in the United States; there are several score small but very powerful establishments. Prisons are scattered geographically and jurisdictionally. Sometimes when a critical problem arises in a prison there is no one to assume final responsibility, no one to criticize for faulty judgment. This happened in New York City in the summer of 1971. It took a week of public investigative hearings to establish that no one inside or outside the city's prison system knew which unit of government or who was responsible for providing life-saving medical equipment to the prison.

Professional Associations
THE AMERICAN CORRECTIONAL ASSOCIATION

The military mentality of the local prison is reflected in the prison establishment's so-called professional associations. All associations of prison personnel are independent affiliates of the American Correctional Association (until 1954, the

American Prison Association). From time to time, in a fit of acrimony, some of the affiliates withdraw from the parent body, only to return after a few years' absence. The American Medical Correctional Association has quit and rejoined more frequently than any other group, perhaps because physicians can satisfy their needs more fully in the American Medical Association. But the American Correctional Association—a loose federation of independent correctional organizations—is only a convenient image-creating device for the prison people. Its primary purposes are to convene an annual conference of all affiliates and to issue public pronouncements advocating the policies cherished by the more powerful affiliates. The Association has but one employee—its General Secretary, and, over the years, has rarely been able to obtain from affiliates sufficient funds to pay office rent in any place for more than a year or two. In 1970, the Association was provided a rent-free, modest unused office at the University of Maryland.

The real sources of power in the prison world are the Wardens' Association and the Sheriff's Association. The other independent affiliates exist only through the suffrance of the wardens and sheriffs for the simple reason that members of the other groups are subordinates of the prison chiefs. They may attend meetings of professional groups only with the permission of their chiefs, they may write articles only with the approval of their superiors, they may criticize prison policies and practices only at the risk of being charged with insubordination.

CHALLENGE . . .

In the last fifty years only one major attempt was undertaken to challenge the power of the prison establishment from within. One of the largest affiliates of the American Correctional Association, the National Council on Crime and Delinquency (until 1960, it was called the National Association of Parole and Probation Officers) undertook, beginning in 1962 a frontal attack on the power center of the establishment. With tremendous energy and generously endowed by millions of dollars from the Ford Foundation, the Council tried to restructure prison management by following a five-pronged strategy:

1. Create a national center to influence both national and local policies regarding prison personnel. The Council succeeded in establishing the Joint Commission on Correctional Manpower. This was accomplished primarily by having Dr. Charles Prigmore, Council staff member, a social worker with many years of experience in prison administration, travel throughout the fifty states lobbying with governors and members of Congress in support of a center to be controlled by the Council. It was understood that Dr. Prigmore was to head it. The Joint Commission was set up in 1965 with Dr. Prigmore as Director. Federal and foundation grants of about $1 million a year were committed.

2. Create in every state of the nation Citizen Advisory Committees to the Council, made up of prominent community leaders who support the Council in its immediate and long-range objectives. The council sent staff members around the country to enlist committee members.

3. Promote close working relationships and affiliations with colleges of social work so as to provide a base of support and influence in the university establishment. It should be noted that nearly all probation and parole agents have degrees in social work. One of the Council's goals was to make social work concepts and practices *the* intellectual discipline of the prison world. The Council sent representatives to the colleges of social work and to national conferences of social work organizations to promote this concept of coalition.

4. Establish a national clearinghouse on research and information on every aspect of prison processes so as to control its development and dissemination. The Council, with public and foundation funds, set up such a center in California in 1965.

5. Generate a public image of the Council as the reliable leader in the prison field. Numerous national conferences were convened by the Council between 1965 and 1970 flooding the news media with press releases concerning safety in the streets, organized crime, delinquency, the courts and prisons.

Between 1965 and 1970, upwards of $7 million were spent to carry out the frontal assault, but the effort proved to be a dismal failure.

Dr. Prigmore, who had done more than anyone else to implement the Council's strategy, was quickly knocked out of his position as the first chief of the Joint Commission on Correctional Manpower. He was replaced by a retired warden, Garret Heyns of Washington. Other social-work staff members of the Commission were dismissed or demoted. Prigmore left to become Dean of the Alabama School of Social Work.

The Council succeeded in setting up only four or five

Citizen Advisory groups; although it could obtain countless names of prominent people for letterheads, few people, busy in their own fields, could afford the time. And the most prominent people in the states were already closely tied up with the "invisible" establishment interested primarily in prison construction. The schools of social work across the nation, which had received, with the urging of the Council, more than fifteen million dollars in federal funds between 1965 and 1970 to train young people for careers in prison work, found that fewer than one per cent of its graduates actually went into prison work. Social work made innumerable claims about what it could do to reform prisons, but its claims were more puff than substance. The Council's Clearinghouse was taken over by the U.S. National Institute of Mental Health; the Council's research center was dissolved; obvious behind-the-scenes maneuvres were hitting away at the Council's effort to take over the establishment.

. . . AND FAILURE

The Council's attempt to promote a public image as *the* center of power for prison change was abortive. It held a widely publicized national conference in 1969 on the "crime crisis" in America—the program listed the names of hundreds of prominent American leaders. The Council expected a thousand concerned conferees. Only a hundred or so invitees turned up, wandering desultorily in the conference halls wondering why they had come.

Since the Council could not succeed effectively in challenging and changing the prison establishment, the Ford

Foundation cut off its financial support of the Council. Unable to pay its rent and staff salaries in several floors of office space in New York City, the Council, in 1971, moved to smaller offices with smaller staff on the donated premises of a New Jersey corporation.

But the wardens and sheriffs are doing fine. Their publications are well endowed with advertisements from steel and armament companies. The costs of their conventions are paid by exhibitors of tranquilizers, electronic surveillance devices, and prison plumbing. Who can challenge this military establishment? By warning that staff demoralization and prisoner riots would result from major reforms, it has successfully fended off the only real attack ever mounted against them. The civilian advisory boards or mandatory prison commissions made up of civilians, of those prisons that have them are hand-picked by prison chiefs and serve only as a rubber stamp for very traditional policies. When a scandal arises, these boards and commissions soothe public opinion, praise officialdom, and back up the perpetuation of the *status quo*.

A UNION THREAT

From behind the prison walls there is only one potential threat to the powers of the baronial potentates. This potential is in the hands of the lowliest but most numerous segment of the establishment, the prison guards. Beginning about 1968, prison guards around the nation began to organize officers' benevolent associations. Reluctant to refer to themselves as labor unions, since many states take a very dim view or are openly hostile to unions of public employees, these associations are, nonetheless, labor organizations. They have sought and gained recognition as bargaining agents for their members in contract negotiations with state executives and legislatures. Quietly, they have begun to explore affiliation with statewide and national labor-union federations. With strength through labor organization they are no longer meekly submissive to the arbitrary demands of their chiefs. They have direct recourse to the governors, the legislatures, and the courts for redress of their grievances. They can even bypass the state prison commissioners and directors who, more often than not, are principally spokesmen for the wardens and sheriffs. State governors who traditionally were reluctant to go against the wishes of a unified establishment, now find a splintering of power—the wardens, sheriffs, and their top management deputies versus a much greater number of increasingly organized prison guards. It does not require much astuteness to recognize that a politician is more likely to be swayed in support of many, organized votes rather than by a handful of wardens, albeit powerful in their fortified domains. As governors and municipal or local chief executives find it more expedient to make concessions over wages, working conditions, and pensions to guards, they will find increasing leverage to expect that guards will make concessions to ideas of prison reform.

The fact that prison guards have begun to create labor unions represents the most significant crack in the walls of the prison establishment in two hundred years. But it will take long for the crack to widen sufficiently for the walls to crumble.

V

THE
STAFF

Rural Conservatism
A PLACE IN THE COUNTRY

Until the enormity of the tragic massacre at Attica exploded in the public's conscience, few people in New York State or the state's capital at Albany or in America had ever even heard of the village of Attica. Few had the faintest notion of where it was located or cared what went on there. Many people have begun to care. More will care as facts of beatings, torture, murders and the inhuman irrationality of the prison establishment are revealed to the American people.

The rural character of most of America's prisons and the fact that nearly all of the guards and administrators in these prisons are themselves rural people helps to explain much of the underlying tension between prisoners and their keepers. Most prisoners—nine out of ten—are in their late twenties and have been born and raised in the major urban centers of the nation. Most of the keepers—six out of ten—are in their late forties (administrators are, on the average, ten years older). There is little communication between staff and prisoners because staff has an active disdain for the big city and have perhaps only visited large cities when attending, at public expense, conferences and conventions of prison personnel. They have little understanding and less appreciation of city dwellers whom they must restrain in custody, supervise, and "correct." A preponderance of the guards in our prisons are older men, former farmers or the sons of farmers forced off the land during the Depression, or they are older men whose aspirations were dashed by having to serve in World War II and lost the opportunity to develop work skills or continue their education. A stable job in prison, gained by political appointment or a civil-service test that required only an eighth-grade reading ability—assured by veteran's job priority —answered many of their life's needs. They could remain in the towns where they had been brought up, keep their homes, own a car, and look forward to a modest tax-supported pension. In return, they had very little to do: maintain discipline, prevent scandals from leaking out to the public, resist any form of change that would rock the boat.

Educate inmates? Rehabilitate them? Train them? Help them? Their jobs do not require that they either believe in such goals or perform in ways to achieve them. Their salaries and pensions do not depend on productivity requiring more than custody. Their lives do not depend on these goals—*yet.*

FRINGE BENEFITS?

Over the years, salaries for the prison establishment have gone up relative to many other salaries for jobs that are essentially unskilled, or at best semi-skilled—jobs requiring little education and mainly physical strength. The benefits of prison jobs are considerable: long vacations, unlimited paid sick leave, free meals, often free portal-to-portal transportation and free car maintenance, easy but illegal access to goods manufactured in prison—and unlimited horizons for theft and corruption.

In Idaho in 1971 prison guards were making deductions from inmates' savings accounts as men left prison. When prisoners asked the reasons for these deductions they were told they could expect trouble if they didn't keep their mouths shut. In South Carolina prison guards have inmates make leather pocketbooks that they sell on the outside, pocketing the profits themselves. In Nebraska and North Carolina prison guards approve the receipt of shipments of food and raw materials for prison factories, but the delivery trucks leave the grounds half full—the profits split by drivers, businesses, and the guards. And there is hardly a prison in the nation in which guards aren't making a profit from the sale of such contraband items as drugs, alcohol, and pornography. Control and elimination of official thievery and corruption is necessary because it is intolerable; but this will not improve the quality of prisons or prison personnel.

In spite of steady work, relatively good pay, and attractive fringe benefits, few city-dwellers enter prison work as a career. Few criminologists want to leave college and university work to practice the ideas they teach in colleges and universities. And although the federal government has spent upwards of eighteen million dollars between 1960 and 1970 to train social workers and teachers for jobs in prison, there were fewer social workers and teachers working in our prisons in 1970 than there were in 1960.

As a result of the total lack of infusion into staff of new blood, new ideas, a youthful approach, prison guards reflect the conservative outlook of those who are cut off from the pressures of changing social conditions. The prison establishment refused to change, partly because they feel more secure behind the walls doing what they have always done, but mainly because there has not yet been a massive demand for change.

Another major source of tension inside prison walls is explained by the fact that 98 per cent of prison guards are white, the remaining 2 per cent are black, Puerto Rican, Mexican-American, and Indian. Nationally, half the prison population is black. In some cities and in some states 60 to 70 per cent of the inmate population is black. Across the nation, an additional 10 per cent of the prisoner population is made up of Puerto Ricans, Mexican-Americans, and Indians. In New York, reflecting the population makeup, 20 per cent of the prisoners are Puerto Rican; in Minnesota 20 per cent are Indian; and in New Mexico 30 per cent are Mexican-American.

Prison guards see blacks, Puerto Ricans, Indians and Mexican-Americans only as prisoners and prisoner visitors, almost never as next-door neighbors, co-workers, or friends. And their life experience, so devoid of contact with minorities who suffer bigotry and discrimination, does not prepare them for any real understanding of minority life. The poor in the United States have always been isolated from the mainstream of American life, isolated in ghetto neighborhoods and schools, isolated in work because they get the menial jobs which keep them in the kitchens and warehouses. In a large city it is difficult to avoid the seething, agonizing, and despairing lives of the poor, but a small-town background can make such avoidance possible. The gap between prisoner and guard is increased because guards by background distrust the ways of the city, and typically prisoners from minority backgrounds are city-bred. There is no communication between guards and prisoners because there is little basis for any.

It is unrealistic to think that merely by training guards to become more aware of the differences between them and their prisoners more sensitive understanding and greater communication will result. Prisons have carried on, since 1960, extensive pre-service and in-service training programs for their guards and administrators. Some of these programs have been carried out in cooperation with universities and specialized commercial training companies. Prison staff has been sent to week-long, sometimes month-long training seminars, workshops, institutes, and have even been provided with semester and year-long leaves of absence with pay to study psychology, sociology, social work, and public administration. Personnel managers from national corporations have conducted classes for prison staff, the educational branches of the federal government has sent in their experts, judges and prosecutors have lectured—all to no avail. At the first National Conference on Correction convened by Attorney General Mitchell in December 1971 at the request of the President, Mr. Mitchell announced the launching of a National Correctional Training Academy, akin to the FBI Academy or to West Point and Annapolis. But this is a bad decision, because training prison staff is not dealing with the central problems of prisons. New York State has operated training programs for prison staff for more than twenty years; in addition, many guards have availed themselves of generous scholarships and stipends to obtain college degrees. The same is true in New Jersey and California. But neither the extensive and costly training or advanced education could prevent the killings at San Quentin, the uprising at the Rahway prison in New Jersey, or the massacre at Attica.

In each of these places as in all the prisons of America, prisoners are being systematically and brutally denied rights that no law or court requires be taken from them. Prison staff does not require training to carry out the law. They have to be told to do so under threat of criminal prosecution. When prison guards and their chiefs contemptuously disregard the law, especially the Bill of Rights, there is no basis for communication with inmates.

What Is the Remedy?

THE COURTS

Inmates have learned a fundamental political lesson, they have begun to demand access for communication to the governor and to the judges of the federal and higher state courts. They have learned that communication has but a single goal

—persuasion. Prisoners cannot persuade prison staff, trained or untrained, about matters of importance. Only governors and judges have the power to persuade and it is to them that lines of communication must be opened and kept open.

Since 1968 judges throughout the country began to abandon their traditional "hands-off" doctrine with regard to prisons—a doctrine holding that under the constitutional philosophy of separation of powers, the executive branch of government could go about running prisons the way it saw fit with only rare intervention by the court in narrowly circumscribed areas. "Hands off" meant ignoring savage beatings of prisoners, denial of the right to see their attorneys or receive mail from them. But deeply troubled by the mounting evidence of stark inhumanity and wholesale injustice, judges began to assert themselves as protectors of the rights of inmates. They held in case after case that the arbitrary punishments meted out to inmates by the prison establishment could be countenanced no longer. In the case of *Sostre v. New York* (U.S. Federal District Court, New York, 1970) Judge Constance Baker Motley ordered the prison establishment to cease all punishment of inmates without giving prisoners a right to air their side of the story in the presence of counsel. Other federal and state judges have gone still further: in Ohio, judges refuse to send convicted people to the Lucas County prison in the belief that it would constitute cruel and unusual punishment, forbidden by the Constitution; a federal judge in New York threatened Attica prison officials with sending in federal monitors to prevent staff brutality against inmates. None of these judges have said in their splendid and far-reaching decisions that staff training contributes to or can eliminate the rottenness of the prison system; specific judicial orders accomplish with minimum time and cost what a generation and millions of dollars have failed to do.

WILL MINORITY HIRING HELP?

It is also unrealistic to expect that hiring guards who are black, Puerto Rican, Mexican-American, or Indian will reduce conflict between guards and prisoners or modify the inhumanity of the prison establishment. Correcting the social balance of prison guards is an impossible task because prison towns make up a society which has few benefits, and which does not welcome minority groups. In many ways, ghetto life is better.

In early 1970 the federal Bureau of Prisons, which operates twenty-six prisons where almost twenty-five thousand prisoners are confined each year, initiated a "three-two-one" hiring policy. That is, prison guards in this federal agency, paying the highest salaries for prison guards anywhere in the United States, would be hired in accordance with the formula: for every three white guards hired, two black and one Chicano would be hired. This policy, seriously and energetically carried out, did not succeed in attracting many black and Chicano job applicants nor did it succeed in preventing more than fifteen serious riots in federal prisons during 1971. For over ten years, the racial balance in the prison system of New York City has fairly reflected the city's population. But this fact did not prevent the numerous bloody insurrections in the city's prisons during 1970 or the continuing homicides, beatings, torture that furnish beleaguered New York City with a prison scandal at least once a month. In Vermont, Maine, and New Hampshire, where the blacks make up less than 1 per cent of the population and there are virtually none of the other minorities, prisons are, practically speaking, made up of all white guards and all white inmates. This social balance did not prevent inmate work stoppages, sit-down strikes and riots during several months of 1971. Nor did this balance prevent the occurrence in New England's prisons of the kinds of brutality, deprivation of rights, and pernicious cruelty that are rampant in every prison of the nation, and have been documented in 1972 by thousands of pages of testimony in Congressional hearings.

It's Only a Job
THE GUARD AT WORK

Prison workers take jobs in prisons for the reasons most workers do—because these are the most available positions. Contrary to the conviction of many critics of our prisons, prison jobs do not attract more sadists and homosexuals than any other type of employment. Most prison workers are married, have children, participate in fraternal and social organizations and religious groups. They spend a lot of time tinkering with gadgets in their kitchens and not, as prison critics like to imagine, contriving instruments of torture in their basement workshops. Many run mail-order businesses to supplement their incomes and, where permitted, hold part-time jobs in addition to prison positions. Because they live in rural areas, many are hunting and fishing enthusiasts. Many are returning to school and earning degrees, some with the hope that advanced education will lead to promotion or the chance to move to another occupation.

Very few enter prison work because of a desire to fulfill a high ideal or to satisfy a professional commitment. Because prison jobs are essentially unskilled work they are easy to get. Jobs are secure, the pay relatively attractive. Beginning salaries for prison guards range from $6000 a year in Delaware to $12,000 in Massachusetts. In general, prison guards earn more than most schoolteachers and college professors, and unlike the teaching profession, prison guards have contrived numerous ways to regularly earn overtime pay.

Prison work is not especially hazardous; injuries and fatalities are a hundred times more frequent in the allied construction industries, fifty times more frequent in the transportation industry, twenty times more frequent in such common laborer's jobs as lumber milling, gravel spreading, truck loading, and ditch digging. Dairy farmers on small independent farms have an accident and fatality rate ten times greater than prison guards and earn on the average only half what prison guards get.

A DEAD END

Although prison work is steady and attractively paid, there is little opportunity for promotion. The number of higher-level jobs in the prison establishment is regulated by state legislative committees, city councils, and budget chiefs in state capitals. Promotion to higher positions is based on longevity of service, occasionally on competitive examinations, most frequently by a combination of the two in addition to having a political patron. There is no way for prison staff to earn more money on their jobs by increased productivity or better performance, like effectively rehabilitating more inmates. There is no way for prison staff to exercise more authority on their jobs except by arbitrary, illegal use of force over inmates. Because they are locked into their jobs like millions of other American workers, prison guards have begun to organize labor unions that advocate higher salary ranges, more overtime pay, additional fringe benefits, and a greater number of higher-level jobs that can be sought through promotion procedures. Often the mere threat of a work stoppage or strike by prison guards will win them concessions by the state government. In 1970, prison guards in New Jersey walked off their jobs for a week. They won most of the demands they sought in spite of the fact that strikes by government workers are illegal. The labor union victory by prison guards in New Jersey has stimulated the establishment of similar unions throughout the nearly 5,000 prison establishments in the country. Illegal strikes by other government employees like teachers, transit workers, postal workers, police, and firemen has given impetus to intensive union organizing among prison workers.

Most people who take prison jobs keep them for life. They stick with their jobs because work conditions aren't bad and, except for the demand that prisoners not escape, their jobs require very little of them. Work in prison is, after all, not too demanding—that is, if you are not a prisoner. Prison personnel easily fall into a rut from which they can be extricated only by retirement or death. In a sense, they are worse off than prisoners, for most will have to spend their lives behind the walls though they've never been arrested nor had to carry a record of criminal stigma for their whole life.

WHO'S TRAPPED?

The real prisoners of our prisons are the guards themselves, and this causes them no end of anguish and anger. Prison guards are part of the mass of millions of American working people, perhaps as much as thirty per cent of the labor force, who are underemployed—locked into their jobs, there is no place to go but down, or out. Much of the anger, potential for violence, and despair that seethes in America today originates from among this mass of workers who have few skills to move ahead, whose limited skills are underutilized, who recognize the moral and intellectual bankruptcy of their work and the putrid swamp of corruption in which they must swim in silence or perish. The atrocious sadism of prison staff is not a genetic urging nor is it nurtured in home or school. It is only part of a job whose limited demands are shaped by walls, isolation, frustration and public indifference.

Prisoners sense the hopeless despair of their keepers and look upon them with contemptuous pity. The public may be inclined to share the attitude of prisoners because the main source of information about prisons comes from the news media which, quite properly, give major attention to the barbarity of prison guards and the corruption of the prison establishment. When the establishment fumes against the news media for not telling about the good side of prisons, reporters ask to be shown these good things, but the answer is silence. There isn't a single mentionable accomplishment prisons can point to. Is it any wonder then that the public neither appreciates nor respects prison employees? It is a tribute to the judgment of the American public that it is reluctant to pour more money down the drain of prison failure. No amount of playing musical chairs with ethnic groups is going to correct the prison situation.

VI

THE
PRISONERS

How They Got There
"CRIMINALS" WITHOUT VICTIMS

About half the people in America's prisons shouldn't be there. They have caused bodily harm to no one; no one's property has been injured. These people have perpetrated victimless crimes. They are drunks, prostitutes, gamblers, vagrants, youngsters who have run away from home, school truants, children whose parents consider them ungovernable, and boisterous adults whom the police grudgingly consider disorderly. These offenses, like homosexuality among consenting adults and drug addiction, embarrass public morals but present no threat to public order.

It is seriously questionable whether there should be criminal laws at all for victimless offenses—and a prison is the very last place in the world to teach morality. In most criminal courts, judges offer moral offenders a choice: a hundred dollars or thirty days. In 1970, nearly a hundred thousand victimless offenders spent time in prison because they couldn't pay a fine averaging a hundred dollars. Rich gamblers pay their fines and go home; petty gamblers go to prison. When corrupt police officers fail to give adequate protection to affluent call girls, the girls are readily able to pay their fines, but not so their streetwalking sisters. Rich drunks never get arrested. And the nearly seven hundred thousand children under eighteen who are sent each year to some type of juvenile prison are from low-income families. Wealthy parents who have difficulties with their children send them to fashionable boarding schools.

Victimless offenders, representing fifty per cent of our annual prison population of over two and a half million people, are really scapegoats for a much larger segment of the American people who commit similar offenses but are not prosecuted or imprisoned for them. For every drunk, prostitute, drug addict, homosexual, truant, or gambler sent off to a lock-up, there are ten who are arrested but not sent away; they are given warnings, placed on probation, acquitted, or have their sentences suspended. For every person arrested for a moral crime there are ten more reported to the police that do not result in an arrest. Many petty crimes, including moral offenses, are never even reported to the police. If the police were to arrest and judges sentence to prison every petty offender our prison population would soar to twenty-five million.

Among the vast number of Americans who commit crimes

against public morals are a few hundred thousand fathers and mothers who commit incest against their children. There are, each year, a few million parents who beat their children so savagely that medical attention, often hospitalization, is required. America's major department stores, about six thousand of them, report that ten to fifteen per cent of their inventories is stolen each year—not by shoplifters but by the stores' otherwise honest employees. Suburban supermarkets and discount houses have installed electronic monitoring devices and hidden windows and are using security guards and trained dogs to ferret out matronly shoppers who pilfer tens of millions of dollars in merchandise.

Scores of thousands of merchants and businessmen fix prices, shortweight customers, adulterate products, produce shabby goods, bribe, corrupt, extort and embezzle—and the victims are mostly the poor. In the name of free enterprise, little is done to mete out justice in ways that would relieve the awesome burden from the backs of the poor. But neither turning the tables around, making the more affluent petty offenders scapegoats for the poor, or locking up all petty offenders under a code of absolute and dispassionate justice will make our prisons work any better.

With rare exceptions, the ones who commit moral crimes are sentenced to prison for less than a year. Forty per cent spend less than ten days, an additional 40 per cent less than six months. While ten days or six months, in principle, is enough time to provide a prisoner with opportunities to learn something of enduring value and to remedy certain health conditions, government leaders and prison officials have been

reluctant to initiate short-term education or training programs. As a result, there are several million moral criminals
in America who spend as much total time as half their adult
lives in prison, with little benefit to themselves and none to
society. Wasted lives and wasted resources are a very high
price to pay for trying to enforce public morals where there
is no injury to either person or property. Prison is not the
place for these people.

THE VICTIMIZERS

The toll on our society the other half of our prison population has taken defies measurement. Nothing can adequately
describe the infamy of their actions in terms of the thousands
of dead, innocent victims of their inhumanity. How can we
possibly calculate grief among survivors, permanent disabilities, perpetual fear? When the Federal Bureau of Investigation estimates that the annual loss through crime is over five
billion dollars it only sketches a crude outline of the worth of
things. The statistic cannot portray the meaning of the loss
to its victims from cherished souvenirs to destruction by arson
and bombing of homes, shops, offices, and factories.

Half of our prison population is made up of violent people.
No amount of philosophy or rhetoric about the inequities of
capitalism, unfairness of courts, or invective against the establishment can weaken the public resolve to respond effectively
to those who trample on the rights of their neighbors and
fellow citizens. The essential issue is not whether or not we
should respond, but how effective our response is. And our
response should not be based on the degree of violence a

criminal uses to carry out his actions; rather, it should begin with how much we know with certainty about what we can do to prevent the recurrence of violence. We should not get lost in a thicket of arguments about whether violent criminals are psychopathic or just plain sick. These arguments concern themselves with issues that are not the underlying problems but only the results, such as whether we have been too tough on hoodlums or not tough enough, whether violent criminals should be treated by psychiatrists or whether we should make greater use of the threat of capital punishment.

Some form of restraint on the freedom of a violent criminal is going to be necessary. The terminology we apply to such restraint is an issue of little importance. What really matters is whether we know what resources and opportunities to make available to such people to help them overcome their violent tendencies, from whatever origins or reasons, and to restore them to useful, peaceful lives. Knowing these people, knowing what motivates them, knowing what will help them join the ranks of tens of millions of law-abiding, essentially peaceful citizens, constitute the immediate challenge.

For about 15 per cent of those we send to prison, we have no answers, no certain knowledge. We know neither why they are violent nor how to help them overcome their violence. Since the chances are considerable that they will repeat their acts of violent depravity, removal from society and confinement is the only reasonable course available. But prisons, as they are presently organized and run, make matters worse for those prisoners whom we don't understand. It actually serves to foster their violence and society has every reason to fear their release.

This 15 per cent is composed of professional murderers, cowardly thugs who kill aged, defenseless people in the course of petty robberies, extortionists who disfigure victims with acid, perverts who mutilate victims of their sexual aggressions, blackmailers, armed robbers, political fanatics who burn, bomb and destroy. The courts of America have not been lenient with these criminals; these offenders get the longest sentences.

This 15 per cent is confined to the rigors of maximum-security prisons, many for twenty-year or lifetime sentences. But even the term "maximum-security prison" does not convey the fact that within such fortresses there are areas of progressively worse deprivation and harsher confinement. The prison establishment fondly calls these areas "maxi-maxi." And within these areas are the medieval dungeons for extreme punishment called "holes," "bings," "boxes," by prisoners. Authorities call these kinds of confinement "disciplinary segregation." Society exacts a full pound of flesh for our most violent, most difficult offenders. But only 1 per cent of them never return to society.

People serving twenty-year, even many serving lifetime sentences, are eventually released under conditions of parole or commutation of their sentences. A twenty-year sentence may require only ten years in prison. In some states, a life sentence may require minimum time in prison of eight years. This 15 per cent constitutes an imminent menace; but different kinds of prisons are required for these people, places where criminal behavior can be studied to facilitate rehabilitation programs.

We have come a long way from indiscriminate capital punishment. In England, a little over a hundred years ago, even fourteen-year-old pickpockets were hanged. We do not send the most violent criminals to remote islands surrounded by shark-infested waters. And we have clearly rejected prison policies authorizing guards to inflict corporal punishment on inmates. Even the most violent and depraved criminal could be transformed into a peaceful, law-abiding and constructive citizen; the challenge is to find under what circumstances this change occurs and how to make it function. Capital punishment hasn't been effective in preventing people from killing. Even the most brutal, isolated prisons haven't prevented new waves of Americans from committing violent crimes. Until we understand how to respond effectively to violent criminals on whom the law places its arm, we are not going to reduce the threat of violent crime. We are only able to deal with the cruel fact that nearly all the violent criminals who have spent time in our prisons have had to participate in rehabilitation programs with the result that on their release they commit many new crimes far more violent and horrific than the ones that got them into prison originally.

Out of a hundred people sent to prison, fifty shouldn't be there, another fifteen cannot be dealt with effectively at the present time—the remaining 35 per cent are essentially not violent. We know enough about the behavior of the last group and how to help them restore themselves to useful lives to know that we are obliged to reform our prisons. This obligation is based on three practical considerations: first, every day that this 35 per cent spends in prison lengthens the time it will take to help them. Second, every day they spend in prison increases the chances that upon their release they will commit a new and more serious crime. Third, every day they spend in prison means a further waste of tax dollars at an increasing rate.

VII

THE NEW
BREED

Forty years ago, the average age of a prisoner was thirty-eight. The average age in 1971 was twenty-six. Most prisoners are better educated than at any time in the past. In 1931, nine out of ten prisoners had less than a sixth-grade education—most were illiterate. Today, almost 50 per cent of all prisoners have had more than a eighth-grade education; 20 per cent have completed high school or gone to college.

There is a growing awareness among prisoners that many aspects of their arrest, trial and imprisonment are patently illegal, representing gross violations of their constitutional rights. Because they are aware they know that events may be shaped by bringing their plight to the attention of the public. By petition and legal review if possible. By testimony about savage beatings and corruption if possible. By dramatic, often tragic events that oblige the public to sit up and listen. And because there are no laws that prohibit prisoners from writing letters to anyone they choose, censorship and withholding prisoners' mail is a practice that is ending. Prisoners have asked for and judges have conceded their right under the first amendment to the Constitution—the right to free speech. It has taken prisoners two hundred years and numerous bloodbaths to win this right.

Because our prisoners have seen young students and lawyers risk their lives and careers in lunch-counter sit-ins, and voter registration drives, they are beginning to reach out to young lawyers, more idealistic and energetic than their predecessors, to talk about their legal and civil rights as prisoners. The establishment has erected powerful obstacles but these are being torn down by judges who vouchsafe prisoners' rights to communicate with their lawyers.

NEW SOURCES OF PRISONERS

Adding to this movement for the demand of rights are the increasing numbers of three groups of Americans who were rarely ever arrested or sent to prison in the past.

The first group: affluent youth, undergraduate and graduate students who have been sent to prison for a variety of crimes committed during the course of political activity. Some of their crimes are relatively minor and inoffensive, like loitering during civil-rights marches and demonstrations, or trespassing while helping labor organizers create unions of migrant farm workers, or disorderly conduct while protesting the war in Viet Nam. Some of their offenses are more serious like burning draft cards, destroying college buildings, setting off bombs and starting fires on the premises of companies that manufacture napalm and other war material. The militancy of these young activists, including a sizable number of priests and nuns, originally was focused on the racial and military policies of the government but has turned, in addition, to the horrific inadequacies of our prisons.

The second group of new prisoners are the children of public figures. Their crimes? Possession and sale of drugs. Smoking marihuana. Indecent and lewd behavior, and countless instances of harassing public officials by acts of vulgarity and downright obscenity. The children of the powerful know the hypocrisy of their parents perhaps better than anyone else and they are not ashamed to talk about this to their fellow inmates. Their parents, on the other hand, concerned lest their youngsters be brutalized in the same manner as bank robbers, murderers, and petty felons and misdemeanants, have been putting pressure on the prison establishment to make life in prison a little more tolerable. The prerogatives of the powerful are beginning, also, to crack the intransigence of the prison establishment.

The other group are veterans of the war in southeast Asia. Because of military service recruitment policies over the past ten years, the military has kept out of uniform those men with prison records, with little education, or with character deficiencies. Draftees are younger, better educated, more aware. Particular awareness has centered on the futility of the Viet Nam war. Many American servicemen have become addicted to drugs—a habit acquired in Viet Nam with heroin purchased from supplies owned by Saigon officials—a drug traffic implicitly protected by the American government. To get drugs—and also under the influence of drugs—servicemen and veterans with no prior criminal records are committing a tremendous number of crimes. In the period 1968–71, military prisons in the United States and overseas increased the number of Americans convicted of serious crimes by almost four hundred per cent. Many veterans are returning home in a period of high unemployment with little hope of getting jobs. The indifference or ingratitude of the American public to the service these men have been required to perform, deep shame for their participation in unconscionable massacres, and for many the added burden of a dishonorable discharge are creating severe obstacles for readjustment to civilian life. These are the veterans who are finding their reward in a prison sentence.

THEY KNOW THEIR RIGHTS

The new prisoners are angry and disgusted. They are familiar with and have openly rejected the hypocrisy and double-talk of military brass, racial bigots, pro-war fanatics, irrelevant university deans and presidents, corrupt and cynical elected officials, and their parents, and they will not accept more of the same from the prison establishment. They have witnessed the destructive forces of their own government at home and abroad, and they recognize that mere talk will not overcome or hold brute force at a distance. College students know of these ugly forces from the killings at Kent State and Jackson Universities. There is a basis for unity between the new types and more conventional types of prisoners. And the massacres at San Quentin and Attica have forged an even broader unity between all types of prisoners and an increasingly enraged public. This unity, bred from violence, has transformed prisons into a highly political issue and prisoners into an articulate and militant political entity. It is truly amazing that America's most deprived, most harassed and punished people, our prisoners, should see fit to ask for reforms reflecting faith in a system of government that has given them little, expressing faith in a society that prefers to ignore them.

VIII

MONEY, SEX, AND POWER IN PRISON

Money

If a businessman were told that a trust fund existed in the United States which was producing no interest, he would probably think that either the fund was too small to produce income or that the managers of the fund were terribly incompetent. Monies held in trust for prisoners amount to about $80 million a year, so the businessman would be wrong on the first assumption but very accurate on the second.

When a prisoner is locked up, any money in his possession is placed in a special account. Any money that he receives—from former employers, from benefits like veteran's pension, or gifts from family or friends—is also placed in the special account. If the prisoner earns any money from work in prison, that money too is held in trust. It is usual in all prisons for inmates to make purchases of sundry items and charge these against his trust account. An average annual amount of about $200 per prisoner is held in the fund—usually called a "commissary account." Considering that the average daily population of our prisons is 400,000 inmates, the total amount that enters the trust fund is about $80 million, although the amount is probably higher than that.

And the money just stays there. It pays no interest, it is not invested. The way the fund is organized and administered represents the most primitive and paternalistic form of control over a person's money. Each day an inmate is allowed to spend a maximum amount on cigarettes, candy, toothpaste, and similar items. The balance of his account simply sits and does nothing for him, for the prison or for the society that sent him there.

With the consent and participation of inmates it should be possible, and would be desirable, to create and run one or more national funds so that the commissary accounts can be put to work. Even if the monies were simply placed in a savings bank paying 5 per cent interest, the income, about $4 million, could be applied to a wide variety of purposes: loans to inmates returning to communities, purchase of law libraries for prisons that don't have them, hiring of lawyers to represent inmates with legal contests against the prison establishment, underwriting the travel costs of families to facilitate more frequent visiting. The fund could probably be harnessed to more imaginative objectives. It could be used, along with governmental and private-venture capital, to finance employment, business, housing, and health services for inmates, released prisoners, and their families. It could be invested in

many ways that would yield more than simple interest from
a savings deposit. But the fund, like the lives of most prisoners, suffers from forced idleness.

MONEY — A POWERFUL FORCE

The control over a prisoner's money is a key establishment
tool for the control of his behavior. Money is a powerful force
in American life; it helps explain much of people's conduct.
And because money is the prime lever for pursuing and ob-
taining the infinite pleasures of life, prisons pay a great deal
of attention to the uses and abuses of money in prison, because it permits officialdom to effectively block access to
pleasure, stifling, at the same time, an inmate's longing for
even the most elementary things.

Inside prison walls, as on the outside, money can buy opportunities; but because opportunities are deliberately controlled so as to be scarce among prisoners, money is subject
to continual connivance and manipulation. Apart from an
urge for sex and power, no motivation other than money has
ever been able to direct the energies or thoughts of prisoners
into less materialistic avenues. Periodic riots calling attention
to abstract ideals of justice are exceptions, but these are short-
lived; when the rubble is cleared, prison life returns to what
the establishment wants to be—an exploitative jungle.

Even America's political prisoners—peace "criminals" and
civil disobedients, about 16,000 of them between 1968 and
1971—who went off to prison with pride and deep commitment to their ideals, found after a while behind bars that
neither discussion nor persuasion and pleas for collective ac-

tion to bring reason and justice into the prisons stirred the masses of prisoners. Although these unusual prisoners were able through reading and writing to sustain their own personal ideals and were respected by fellow inmates, they found themselves isolated—not because they represented a threat to the prison establishment but because fellow inmates found them without anything tangible to offer. The lofty aims of social justice provides no relief from the rigors of solitude and isolation. But relief *can* be gotten quickly—with money— through contraband drugs, whiskey, and sex.

In our society, which is based primarily on a money economy, all social relationships are affected by a concern with money: the noblest philanthropy and the most infamous larceny have that in common. A generation of research on family relationships has consistently found that money is the chief cause of discord between husband and wife, between parents and children; the source of these tensions is not how much money there is, but who has the power to control its uses.

The perverse practices with regard to money in prisons are not going to be eliminated simply, either by doing away with the money system there or by making more money available to prisoners. The solution lies in finding more effective ways to provide prisoners with better access to money, greater value for the goods and services that money buys, and freedom to determine how their money is to be used.

There is no difference in principle in the money inequities found in prison and those on the outside. The real difference is one of degree. The billions of dollars spent in the nation's "war on poverty" accomplished pitifully little, not because the money was insufficient to reduce poverty, but because fierce power struggles arose among competing groups of poor people and between these groups and local governments over control of the poverty-war chest.

EVERYTHING MONEY CAN BUY

No prison in the nation can stave off accusations that prison personnel are corrupt. Congressional hearings on prison conditions over the decade 1960–70 have produced more than 100,000 pages of documents reciting a long litany of specific instances of the systematic corruption of prison personnel. At these hearings, inmates and former inmates alike testified that, for a price, anything could be bought in prison. In every American prison inmates wih money can get their linens changed daily, get easy work assignments, special food and drink, more frequent visits and mail, and special cell accommodations—often with a high-priced call girl. Some imprisoned professional gamblers are allowed, for a price, to continue their betting operations on the prison telephone or by hiring guards as couriers to the gambling network on the outside. In spite of the vast swamp of corruption and public testimony to corroborate it, few scandals have erupted because of it, few changes have been made.

Gambling flourishes in every prison of America—not as a pastime to while away the long hours and days but as a necessity which according to the laws of chance, may help to equalize an inmate's prospects for corrupting his easily corruptible keepers. Gambling debts among prisoners are paid promptly, either by payment of commissary items or by deposit of the amount owed into the winner's personal account. Where transfer of money between inmates is prohibited, the debts are paid to a friend or relative of the loser who, in turn, mails the money to the winner.

Losers who do not have the means to pay debts are obliged to turn to prison loan sharks—some are prison personnel; most are other inmates—or they turn to stealing or become paid informers of the prison establishment and other law-enforcement agencies. Thefts often involve prison property—stolen by inmates, removed and sold by personnel, and the profits divided. The life and work of a paid informer is not difficult but it is very complex. Conflicting demands are made on him by both officialdom and inmates; he is often a double agent and trusted by none. His work generates fear and suspicion, and in time he becomes a liability and is "liquidated" —sometimes by inmates, sometimes by guards. The thousands of deaths that occur in our prisons each year are rarely investigated; routine autopsies often cover up violent homicides by a report of suicide or death from natural causes or a work accident. The perverse money system of our prisons explains many killings.

Prisoners without money are prey to every conceivable degradation at the hands of other prisoners and with the tacit approval and complicity of personnel, if not at the hands of personnel themselves. Money means survival, it means ability to compete and to corrupt. Collection of prison debts is often deferred until an inmate is released and can participate in a new crime to make good on his obligations. Some become paid informers even before they are sent to prison. Every law-enforcement agency in the nation maintains a special fund to hire informers.

Affluent prisoners, on the other hand, run the prisons. Their money is able to affect the day-to-day operations and the system of privileges on which these operations are based. They are needed by the establishment to lubricate the system's cynicism and hypocricy; they are needed by their fellow inmates who cannot beat but can only accommodate to the system. The affluent also maintain their position of strength by providing philanthropy to inmates who, because of extreme indigency, advanced age, sickness, or mental deficiency, could not survive on their own. Incapable of stealing from other inmates, untrustworthy for postprison crimes, cut off from outside financial help, these inmates provide their affluent fellow with a base of popular support and loyalty, and reciprocate charity with small favors: cleaning, running errands, or taking the blame for infractions committed by their social superiors.

It would be foolish to attempt to rid prisons of the pernicious money system by regulation. No society has been able to rid itself of vice through legislation. A parallel money system along the lines of the money system found outside of prison would do much to relieve the horrendous exploitation that goes on in prison. Sound economic alternatives would lessen the stranglehold of corruption.

When tragic riots erupted at the Attica prison, the first demand expressed by the prisoners was for a plan of minimum wages for work performed in prison. It was not a new demand, nor one that has been advocated solely by prisoners. It is a problem that has been on the minds of people concerned with prisons for a long time. In 1970, the fifteen members of President Nixon's Task Force on Prisoner Rehabilitation recommended instituting minimum-wage programs in all the nation's prisons.

In part, the recommendation was made in recognition of the desirable impact it would have in providing incentives to the prison establishment to bring modern industrial and business practices into prisons as a vital aid in helping offenders ready themselves for independence. Also responsible was the conviction that the concept of involuntary, unpaid labor was no longer tenable, that deprivation of a man's liberty was society's principal vengeance for the harm done, but that deprivation of liberty was no justification for preventing a man from earning a living even in confinement.

Nothing happened to implement the Task Force's recommendation; hence it is not surprising that after two hundred years of exploited labor in American prisons, the issue finally was internationally dramatized not by distinguished civilian experts but by the victims of the system themselves. Attica's prisoners were not asking for an end to prisons, only for a beginning of economic independence.

A valuable first step would be enactment by Congress of an amendment to the minimum wage laws calling for minimum wages to be paid to inmates of all federal, state, and local prisons. This would serve two immediate purposes. The first would be provision of the means for prisoners to earn money, to be paid adequately for the work they do while in prison. The second would be provision of opportunities for spending the money earned in ways that directly relate to the reasons why we have prisons in the first place: to protect people and property from harm and to assist the offender in restoring himself to a useful life.

SPENDING MONEY USEFULLY

Through Congressional enactment of a minimum-wage provision for prisoners, four kinds of spending opportunities should be encouraged: reparations, payment of court and prison costs, family support, and free investment. Some might be mandatory; it would be preferable if all were voluntary.

The most important would be the possibility for payment of reparations to victims of crime. It should be possible to introduce changes in court sentencing procedures so that the length of time of a sentence is affected by how long it takes an offender to make reparations to a victim. Current prison policies result in a reduction of prison time based on good behavior—so many days less time to serve for so many months of good behavior. But this is a rigid, paternalistic method that should be abandoned. For what is "good" behavior in prison has no realistic meaning outside the walls. The "good" prisoner acquiesces to inhuman demands, force, corruption, violence, and hypocrisy. There is much decency in most prisoners, for eventually most abandon the spurious "good" prison standards in favor of the more flexible and meaningful standards of the community. Reduction in prison time or in any other form of restraint should be based on a scaled reduction in the harm that has been perpetrated—a modern, more reasonable and compassionate equivalent of the "eye for an eye, tooth for a tooth" philosophy.

The concept of reparations, by its very nature, obliges the person making reparation to perceive natural rules of equity in the relationships among men, and the inherent human injustice in any form of exploitation. Pay incentives for prison work based on increased skills, increased work responsibility, increased productivity would have a direct relationship to a prisoner's motivation for reducing the prison sentence through accelerated reparation payments. Earned "good" time serves no purpose for society other than preserving a false semblance of superficial order in the conduct of prison affairs.

A second kind of spending opportunity involves the purchase of court and prison services. In effect when a person commits a crime he obliges society to pay the costs for a trial and his imprisonment. Not only is the victim of his crime deprived of his rights, property, peace of mind, and integrity of body, but the crime increases the burden of tax-supported public services. Prisoners should be provided wih opportunities for paying these costs or at least a portion of them through income taxes deducted from prison earnings or through a combination of taxes on prison earnings and direct payments for court and prison costs. A reduction of sentence or prison time should also be possible on the basis of payments of public costs by the inmate and tied directly to the inmate's ability to earn.

Other services that prisoners should be given an opportunity to pay for are education, recreation, food, clothing, and other personal items including amenities associated with room furnishings. The public should not object to a prisoner's purchase of such goods and services as it will cost the public nothing. On the contrary, the reform of the prison money system would result in substantial reduction and eventual elimination of public tax costs for most prisons. Revenues from inmate taxes and inmate spending would help to curb the mounting costs for law-enforcement services in general. If an offender is to pay for his crime, we first have to provide him with the means to do so.

A third type of spending opportunity for prisoners involved contributing to family support. Forty per cent of the nation's prisoners are married and have children. When a family man is sent to prison the chances are considerable, although there is no hard information about the numbers involved, that his family must turn to some form of public assistance. Whether the nation's much and justly criticized welfare program is overhauled and replaced by a better system or supplanted by guaranteed minimum family income, there is no reason why a prisoner with the opportunity to earn wages should not also have the opportunity to contribute to the support of his family.

The primary objective of financial contributions to family support ought not be the reduction of the burden of public dependency of prisoners' families. Instead, the goal ought to be the fostering of continuity of family ties in the most ancient and fundamental way—by providing shelter, food, and clothing through one's personal efforts. Our present system discourages any form of family continuity and it cost us more than two billion dollars in 1971 to make sure that our prisoners would not be gainfully employed and could not support their families. The additional advantage to the public in having prisoners assume all or most of the costs for supporting their families increases the need to provide prisoners with minimum-wage employment.

Of the sixty per cent of our prisoners who are single, little is known about their families or about their need for support. Doubtless, many prisoners have parents who become dependent upon public assistance when a court imposes sentence. Such offenders should be given the means to support their parents. Much more is known (but without precise statistical information) about the large number of unmarried prisoners who, between prison terms, become fathers of illegitimate children. Of the 300,000 illegitimate babies born each year in America, it is probable that at least one out of five owes his paternity to a man who has just been released from prison and who, during the birth and early years of the child, is sent back to prison. An effort should be made to identify the fathers of these children, and they should be obliged to contribute to the support of their children. This is a policy that is applied to nonprisoners; it should also apply to prisoners.

A fourth kind of opportunity for spending earnings from minimum wages consists of the many ways that ordinary citizens try to enhance their capital: through interest-bearing savings accounts, investment in stocks, bonds, and businesses, and where gambling is legal to try their luck on lotteries, dog and horse races, and gaming tables. Since gambling cannot be prevented, allowing prisoners to gamble where it is legally permissible would have the effect of reducing the threats of intimidation and the blackmailing of inmates who are not able to pay off gambling debts incurred in prison.

Sex
PERVERSION AND DEPRIVATION

The perverse money economy in prison leads to inexpressible sexual perversity. The youngest, poorest inmates are frequently victims of rape. For money, prisoners allow themselves to become male prostitutes as they allow themselves to act as guinea pigs for drug-company experiments. Some inmates who are raped literally lose their minds, others attempt suicide. Some inflict wounds on themselves in order to be transferred to a hospital where there is less chance that they will have to be coerced into some new sexual humiliation. This is all done with the knowledge of prison personnel; many are paid for their complicity. The origin of the sexual aberrations that pervade all our prisons for the very young as well as for adults is to be found in the organization of our prisons.

Prisoners are denied opportunities for sexual expression because of the nature of confinement rather than because a judge decrees that a sentenced person shall be subject to sexual denial and deprivation. No state or federal law has ever been passed requiring that as a condition of prison confinement a person shall be denied the right of sexual expression. If such a law were ever passed or were a judge ever to deliver such a sentence, the action would be quickly declared unconstitutional. But such laws don't have to be proposed or considered by legislatures because sexual denial takes place automatically along with the many other deprivations that are not specified under law.

Criminally violent homosexuality is widespread in prisons and condoned by officialdom because it constitutes still another area of behavior for arbitrary control and exploitation by the establishment. Those who commit forced attacks bribe their keepers to overlook the rules; the victims must bribe their keepers for protection and possible reassignment of cells. If consensual homosexuality among prisoners were legal, the prison establishment would find ways to circumvent the law since voluntary consent about anything in prison is intolerable to the mind of the establishment. In 1971 the Canadian government enacted a law which permits acts of homosexuality among consenting adults when performed in private. But the law did not extend to prisons, and the justification was that prisons are not private places. Were the same laws to be passed in the Unted States, the prison establishment would lead the protest against making the protections of the law available to prisoners, and they would argue that homosexuality leads to a breakdown in discipline. But the exact contrary has been the case: unofficial toleration of homosexuality has given the guards more forceful control over inmates and has given them substantial illegal profits as well.

Any newspaperman can readily report numerous instances of homosexual rape and obligatory male prostitution in prisons, even in prisons located in the hearts of big cities and close to public awareness. But the stories, unless they are likely to embarrass a public official around election time, are not considered newsworthy.

In 1968 a scandal rocked Philadelphia; it was not just another story of homosexual rape or a gang attack on a new inmate. What was different about this story is that the rape occurred within minutes after the judge delivered a sentence and while the inmate was being transferred in a sheriff's van from the court to the prison—in the presence and with the full knowledge of officers of the court. A full-scale investigation was launched by the District Attorney's office and reports were duly produced. The investigations did not prevent subsequent rapes of young prisoners, whose attempts to complain to prison officials were met with taunts and threats.

In 1969 several women prison officers at New York City's women's prison were dismissed when it became known that they were paying inmates with favors for homosexual acts; it attracted hardly any public attention, notwithstanding the fact that the prison officers had acted as sexual aggressors.

In 1970, as the prison riot season began, many prison officials discontinued their practice of extorting bribes from aggressive inmates bent on rape for fear that allegations of their corruption would worsen the riots when they inevitably occurred.

PROSTITUTES AVAILABLE

In the absence of specific laws about sexual expression, some prison officials have set up private visiting rooms for prostitutes to provide sexual services to inmates who can pay the price. A percentage is paid to the officials. In some states, prisoners with means are allowed temporary freedom for as long as it takes to find a sexual partner. Occasionally, a reported escape of a prisoner is little more than a case of an inmate who fails to return to his cell on time after a sexual caper outside the walls. In the vicinity of some major state prisons, there are rows of brothels whose clients are primarily inmates who pay their keepers for the privilege of a brief outing to find sexual gratification.

In a growing number of prisons conjugal visiting is permitted. This practice involves provision of a bedroom and sufficient time for an inmate to preserve patterns of sexual intimacy with a spouse, a pattern that would normally have been terminated by a sentence. But conjugal visiting is reserved for prisoners who officialdom defines as "good"—if he is an especially "good" prisoner, his female visitor does not have to prove she is the inmate's spouse. Some communities condone sexual visitations; some are openly hostile; most are indifferent. It is the same kind of indifference expressed towards homosexual rape.

In many states that permit daytime release of prisoners for the purpose of finding and keeping a job, work-release practices involve little effort on the part of prison personnel to find jobs. For many inmates "work" release is little more than a thinly disguised excuse to find sexual partners. What is most to be criticized about this practice is not that it helps to reduce some of the tensions of prison life, but that it becomes an additional form of manipulation and control in the hands of prison officialdom.

THE GUARD AS PIMP

One of the worst forms of official and corrupt exploitation of the sexual lives of inmates has been described at the Holmesburg prison in Pennsylvania. The practices are not unique to that state. At Holmesburg, prison management successfully tied the sexual needs of inmates to the vicious money system in the prison. Inmates with money to pay guards are allowed their choice of sexual partners from the prison population. Inmates who serve as informers may also choose sex partners for either a private or gang rape. Reluctant inmates who refuse to comply with these arrangements are punished by prison staff with beatings or transfer to isolation. Enforcement of this sex-money economy is brought about by threat of mutilation or death; the torturers are either guards or prisoners. Victims know they can do little to prevent the dire consequences of resistance.

To assure access to money so that the economy may function smoothly, guards in Holmesburg—and in many other large prisons—covertly arrange with drug companies to provide inmate subjects for testing new and dangerous drugs. Token amounts are paid to inmates, giving them the means to buy sex; larger amounts are paid to prison staff for their cooperation. Inmates are eager to participate in dangerous drug experiments, recognizing that they have been specially selected by their captors as good prospects for taking part and trustworthy in keeping quiet.

REASONABLE SEXUAL EXPRESSION

The sexual life of most people in western society is regulated, more or less, by community standards and levels of education. Society provides no assurances and few formal means for an individual to find that form or frequency of sexual expression that best corresponds to his personality or his need of intimate relationships whether homosexual or heterosexual. Young people, the elderly, the infirm and handicapped, and those who are confined to institutions are all especially vulnerable to sexual deprivation as a practical matter rather than as a result of formal codes of behavior. Very short people, unusually tall, bald, plain-looking, or very shy people probably have many complaints about sexual expression that are as valid as any other, but five thousand years of civilized society have not made the sexual lives of these people any better; whatever formal or informal rules for sexual conduct exist are honored more in the breach than the observance. The only type of sexual behavior that can and should be prevented by civilized society is forceful violation of one's sexual privacy—rape, whether homosexual or heterosexual.

Prisons have proven unable to deal meaningfully or effectively with sexual expression without resorting to jungle warfare. The only kinds of sexual expression permitted or encouraged by the prison establishment are those that enhance the establishment's power, at the same time fostering among inmates a cynical disregard for law, privacy, and individual dignity. The techniques of violence are needed to preserve the sex-money system; society's need to eliminate this source of violence far outweighs any type of benefits for the select few.

For as long as we continue to need prisons, prisoners should be allowed periodic leaves or furloughs, as a matter of right rather than as purchased favor or under the guise of an evasive work or educational release. Most of our present prison population pose no threat of violence in the community, and furloughs would allow them to find their own level in all facets of community life including sexual expression. Government intervention that permits sexual visitation only for married prisoners is highly discriminatory against those whose preferred form of sexual expression is homosexuality and is equally discriminatory against unmarried prisoners.

CONJUGAL VISITS

When, in 1970, the New York State legislature convened public hearings to consider the possibility of enacting laws to make conjugal visiting possible, legislators were deluged by protests. Paradoxically, neither religious, political, nor humanitarian groups made the protests; it was the wives of prisoners themselves. They complained vehemently that visits to their spouses that included the possibility of sexual relations was personally humiliating and grossly demeaned the emotional aspects of sexual expression. The proposed laws were promptly shelved.

But California, New Jersey, Texas, North Carolina, and many county-run prisons have, since 1968, set up cottages for inmate residence where prisoners may receive spouses or people to whom they are engaged to be married. Rules in these prisons are flexible, and to offset the expected complaints of homosexual inmates, officialdom is tolerant of homosexuality.

There are several big problems associated with prisons whose policies regarding sexual expression might be considered "flexible." First, these prisons, many set up as experiments, tend to receive from other prisons a very select group of inmates who in the opinion of prison officials are likely to comply with the prison administration's *ad hoc* rules regarding sexual conduct. The selection of inmates for these places is not based on what the community expects or demands or what laws expect or demand. Second, these prisons operate on the basis of arbitrary decisions made by officials. Officials are free to abandon the "flexible" practices at will and in the prisons where selection is made for transfer of inmates to "flexible" settings, inmates tend to become even more docile and submissive in complying with the demands of their captors in order to receive favorable consideration. But since the practices of "flexible" prisons come very close to the largely unregulated behavior as regards sex in the free community, they should be made an integral part of prison life for most prisons for as long as we continue to find them necessary. And prisons will be necessary as long as violence continues to be a part of American life.

Candid recognition of the sexual rights of prisoners and allowing these rights to be pursued would not turn prisons and nearby communities into bordellos or produce mass sex orgies. The sex-money economy of prisons has accomplished this already and the recognition of inmates' sexual rights would swiftly end much of the horror of the current practices.

For spouses, sweethearts, common-law partners, and intimate friends who do not find visiting that includes sexual expression a demeaning experience, such visitation should be allowed. For those whose mode of sexual behavior is homosexual, homosexual relations should be permitted both among consenting prisoners as well as with homosexual partners from outside of prison. For those whose only means for finding sexual expression is through the payment of prostitutes, male or female, prostitutes should be allowed to practice their occupation—as in Nevada where prostitution is legal and regulated by health agencies, or as it is in those states and cities where laws against prostitution are not enforced but where efforts are made to prevent venereal disease. Prisoners allowed to work and paid decent wages for their work should be allowed, if they desire, to maintain a semblance of normal sexual expression—it is for most people too fundamental a need to be allowed to become a tool of official repression.

But what of those whose behavior is too violent? What of those who, notwithstanding "flexible" rules, are violent aggressors? What of their need to satisfy sexual urges and longing for intimate social contact? For those men and women for whom confinement is essential until they mature out of violence or until society understands violent behavior well enough to control and curb it, the answer is social isolation —but isolation not in the traditional prison meaning of solitary confinement in grim, airless cells with short rations, but social isolation without physical deprivation, where work and study may continue, where recreation and rest may continue, where the ability to communicate by writing is not impaired. For violent offenders social isolation is indispensable, but without infringement of basic rights or conveniences other than the right to intimate social contact and sexual expression with others.

Power
RACISM

The control of money and the control of sex are the chief sources of power in prison, but there are others. Many of the power relations in prison among inmates and between inmates and prison personnel continue traditional forms of exploitation found outside of prison. White prisoners with the support and encouragement of predominantly white guards exercise tremendous influence over the behavior of black and other minority inmates. Black prisoners and the other minorities get the worst cell assignments, the hardest work, the most menial tasks. Until the riots of 1970–71, many of which entailed full-blown racial confrontations, hundreds of prisons, North and South, required black inmates to wear white gloves when they served officers and white prisoners. Where there are many Mexican-American, Puerto Rican, and Indian inmates, sordid methods for the humiliation of these groups are employed. Contempt, patently discriminatory assignments, and arbitrary punishment for real or imagined infractions of prison rules are used to assert and maintain the traditional social superiority of the white prison elements —inmates and officialdom.

Where there are education and training programs, the nonwhite minorities are often excluded because prison personnel say that they lack the minimum qualifications to enter such programs. Where there are work-release programs and furloughs, the numbers of nonwhites who are allowed to take part is kept at a minimum because officials contend that they represent a high risk in the community and that their prison records show a lack of willingness to cooperate with authorities. Nonwhites are most frequently the victims of beatings, most frequently their deaths in prison are reported as "suicides," and they are most frequently defendants in the prison kangaroo courts dominated by white inmates. They are also most often the victims of rape and other sexual aggressions.

MONEY AND MAFIA
CONNECTIONS HELP

Many inmates and former prisoners contend that the real power of prison life is controlled by a coalition between white officialdom and white "mobbies." The mobbies are reputedly members of white criminal gangs, syndicates, and whatever remains of local Mafia organizations. The mobbies have plenty of money available; many continue loan-shark operations in prison along the lines that brought them into prison in the first place. Because of their access to money, they are able to do favors for prison personnel, bribe them, even help them find new jobs when they tire of prison work. The mobbies are skilled operators and know how to organize and carry out, with establishment cooperation, distribution of contraband drugs, alcohol, and pornography. Mobbies, moreover, get more favorable consideration for early release under parole, for the establishment argues that since they have money, a job, a family, a home, they more adequately meet the arbitrary standards for favorable parole consideration.

Individual prisoners who are rich or who may have had powerful political connections on the outside are respected by inmates, but social contact between them is minimal because of the apprehension on the part of rich prisoners that deeper involvement in their day-to-day lives may lead to public exposure and an end to the adjustments made possible by corruption. Their assessment is realistic, for a prisoner who is a former congressman, judge, or captain of industry is not likely to have much influence since his former associates and contacts will not jeopardize their own situations as long as he remains in prison.

Much of what goes on in prison, day by day, is determined by those prisoners who have money, who have underworld connections, or who are outspoken and ready violently to defend their conviction in white racial supremacy. (The importance of racial bigotry as a criterion of power is, however, probably diminishing in those prisons where the number of minority prisoners is increasing and where younger minority prisoners become violently defiant in the face of intimidation and debasement based on race.) In some prisons the most powerful inmates—or gorillas and wiseguys, as prisoners call them—have to possess more than money to be respected and allowed to exercise their power. Often underworld connections is the additional element that establishes their supremacy, for many inmates need outside connections for future credit and illegal assignments. The prison establishment is part and parcel of these power arrangements: it helps get things done for them, it helps preserve and cover up the awful exploitation of labor, it has helped keep prisoners docile, and the arrangements are profitable.

SELF-GOVERNMENT AS AN ANSWER

A drastic change in the money-sex economy of prisons would go a long way towards breaking up the internal power arrangements from which the establishment derives so much of its power to perpetuate its system of ruthless coercion and corruption. A parallel money system would do much good by itself; so would relaxation of sex rules—and a combination of both would help transform prison autocracies into centers where the methods of democracy, albeit imperfect, can be practiced. Eventually the totalitarian power of prison people will be replaced by viable patterns of inmate self-government. Until inmates have legal access to money and legitimate opportunities to express sexual longings, there is little for self-government to govern.

Reorganization of power in prisons must provide for meaningful participation of inmates in setting prison policies and in carrying them out. The best reorganization would require elimination of prison guards, officials, and other prison personnel—except for a staff sufficient to make the community secure in its knowledge that violent men have the necessary degree of restriction on their movement. Apart from explicit restrictions required by security, inmate self-government would allow inmates to hire or contract—with their own earnings—the kinds of specialists, technicians, and staff they themselves consider to be most appropriate for the lives they must lead while in prison. This would do away with the long-held and ill-founded belief of many that social workers or psychiatrists are best able to rehabilitate prisoners. Very convincing research evidence has proven this belief to have been a very costly mistake.

Making their own choices, prisoners are likely to select those specialists who can provide them and their families with tangible help rather than merely trying to implement current fashions in individual or group therapy. Inmates might, quite probably would, want to hire energetic and competent teachers of academic and vocational subjects rather than to rely on the low-paid and low-prestige teachers who now refer to themselves as "correctional educators." They might—probably would—want to hire outstanding experts from industry and business to train them in the modern ways of overcoming their many job limitations and lack of perspective on future opportunities for earning a living. There is something terribly wrong, even indecent, in training prisoners for jobs that exist only in prison, no longer exist, or will disappear in the near future—a common practice in all prisons. Genuine inmate self-government—power exercised by those whom the courts say must be temporarily restrained in their free movement—would permit them to make decisions on their own and not have decisions spoon-fed by narrow-vision prison establishmentarians who don't want to be bothered by anything more than keeping inmates locked up and docile—at present, their sole obligation to the community.

Prison rules for conduct determined by inmates would more nearly and intelligently correspond to the needs of men rather than to the capricious demands of a military bureaucracy primarily concerned with expendable numbers. When inmates are given the means to behave democratically they will more readily accept and act on greater challenges—to work, to learn, to cooperate—without which democracy is an illusion.

IX

JOBS
AND
EDUCATION

Jobs

When Congress set up the U.S. Bureau of Labor (later, Department of Labor) in 1884, one of the least-known provisions of its broad mandate was to conduct, at ten-year intervals, a comprehensive survey of work performed, working conditions, and wages paid to prisoners in every prison of the nation. In nearly ninety years of Labor Department history, only four surveys were actually undertaken as required. The first three—in 1885, 1895, and 1923—were superficial and incomplete inasmuch as they looked at only federal prisons and the largest state penitentiaries. The fourth and last survey was completed in 1932, and is the only study to comply with the demand of Congress that it examine *all* prisons of the country. A stern indictment of our prison practices, the report on prison labor didn't get more attention than publication in an obscure statistical bulletin published by the Labor Department; the Great Depression and the "recovery" administration of Franklin Roosevelt turned the nation's attention to more immediate problems. The document is remarkable in demonstrating how little our prisons have changed in forty years.

In the largest prisons, according to the 1932 report, barely one half of the inmates were engaged in any kind of work; in smaller state, county, and city prisons seventy per cent of the inmates were reported "sick or idle." In 1932 when our total prison population was about 159,000, the total value of goods produced by prison labor was $75 million, or about $500 of value produced per inmate. Money paid to prisoners ranged from two cents to "not more than" fifteen cents per day. And the report tells that the prisoners who worked (22 per cent of the total) were obliged to put in more than sixty hours a week of labor. State prison inmates worked over sixty hours a week in Alabama, Georgia, Louisiana, Mississippi, and North Carolina; in Texas the work week averaged more than seventy hours.

Except for inmates of federal prisons, the situation in 1971 was better in some prisons but worse in most. In federal prisons about thirty per cent of the inmates are allowed to work for "incentive" payments that average about thirty-five cents an hour, with a maximum earning of twenty dollars per month. The total value of goods manufactured in *federal* prisons in 1970 was about $50 million, about $1800 of value produced for each of the 24,000 inmates in the federal system. There is no way of knowing exactly the value of goods produced in thousands of other prisons, but the "incentive" payments range from five to thirty-five cents per hour with maximums ranging from five to twenty dollars per month.

Prison officials testifying before Congressional committees have estimated that the inmates who work represent between ten and fifteen per cent of the total prison population. The 1932 report on prison labor noted that the situation in that year was worse than in 1923 and that 1923 was worse, in terms of idleness, than 1885. Were a survey to be undertaken in 1972 the report would probably conclude that the situation now is worse, considerably worse than it was almost ninety years ago.

The unemployment rate among people being released from prison is at least three to four times higher than it is among the general working-age population. Unemployment among offenders from black and other racial minorities is twice that of nonoffenders from the same groups. But this is only an estimate. No one knows exactly how many people in America have no jobs, since unemployment figures ignore those who, in sheer despair have given up the search for work.

After the tragic city riots of 1967, the Census Bureau and the Labor Department sent teams of researchers into the inner-city neighborhoods where the riots had erupted. The researchers went into places where the regular ten-year census enumerators had never gone: bars, bowling alleys, poolrooms, flophouses, third-rate restaurants. And they counted people who had never been counted before. They found people, many of them in their late teens or early twenties, who had never before worked on either a full- or part-time basis. Obviously these could not be counted in official unemployment statistics based on people receiving unemployment-insurance payments. These were the invisible unemployed: some of them believed that they would never find jobs, pointing to their neighborhoods in which 25 per cent of all able-bodied people had been unemployed for as long as ten years; others reported that they were not looking for work because of prison records—fully aware that their color, inexperience, and their records would probably bar them from most jobs.

What the survey of the invisible unemployed revealed was that the actual unemployment in slum neighborhoods, in areas where riots had occurred, was actually three to four times higher than had been officially reported earlier. It was found, for example, that out-of-school youth in these neighborhoods had an unemployment rate of close to 40 per cent as contrasted with the earlier official tally of 10 to 12 per cent. The unemployment rates for older people was even more discouraging for people who believe that things in America weren't too bad or that conditions were getting better. Men in the prime of life, between thirty-five and forty-four, across the nation experienced an unemployment rate of only 2 per cent; but when the invisible jobless men of this age were included in the figures the rate leaped to 8 per cent—and for married offenders in this age bracket, the figure rose to almost 16 per cent.

For a long time the American public accepted the claims of the prison establishment that prisoners performed useful labor and that prisons were equipping them for useful work on release. It is high time that this claim be recognized for what it really is—a callous lie. To continue to accept this deception means that we will continue to pour billions of dollars a year down a bottomless hole. To change the situation we must begin to examine the problem of inmate manpower in the larger context of American manpower.

Much of the talk centering on unemployment in the 1960s was concentrated on the problems of either the people who had been kept out of the job market because of discriminatory practices of employers or regions of the country that had been especially hard hit by joblessness because of the shutting down of major industries. The former, referred to as the hard-core unemployed, had the highest rates of unemployment in America because most of the group had had only an eighth-grade education, had few or no marketable job skills, a spotty record of previous work mainly in menial part-time jobs, a family background of strained financial means—generally dependence on public welfare—and residence in a slum neighborhood. And if these exclusionary barriers weren't enough, employers argued that this group was "unmotivated" to work, couldn't get to work on time, and had a tendency to quit a job after only a few weeks or months of employment.

Congress tried to rectify the situation with the passage of the Manpower Development and Training Act of 1962. Beginning that year the law, backed up by billions of dollars plus pressures on employers to open the doors to the "hard core," many became employed. Business and industry accepted generous federal dollar incentives that paid for training of this group; unions cooperated by encouraging union membership, lowering, at the same time, traditional union barriers for membership. Commissions, courts, and community groups mounted mass protests to get jobs for the persistently unem-

ployed minorities. Entrance tests for new workers, like quali-
fying tests for new voters, were shown up to be pure sham,
and under protest, the tests were abandoned. Employers with
minority personnel working at higher than entrance-level jobs
were pressured to promote them to higher level positions so
as to create promotion opportunities for entering minority
workers. The Manpower Act provided training for those with
few or no job skills, weekly, decent stipends for those with no
money, counseling and health services for those that needed
them. Some of the vast spending was politically calculated to
keep slum youth off the streets in summertime to reduce the
possibility of rioting, and it helped. Some of this historic effort
was calculated to distribute money to the poor as a supplement to welfare and to prevent the welfare rolls from swelling.
Some of the spending and effort resulted in tens of thousands
of decent jobs that promised opportunity and a bright future.

But a closer look at the successes of the Act reveals that it
barely scratched the surface of providing aid to those hundreds of thousands for whom job barriers were most impene-
trable: people with arrest and prison records. Federal and
state labor department officials say they do not know the
extent to which manpower programs included or excluded
offenders, but they concede that virtually no offenders were
provided the benefits of job training, stipends, or the other
vital assistance envisioned by Congress. There are still millions of people, especially young people, who are destined to
spend much of their adult years without jobs, without salable
job skills, and without any prospects of ever getting and holding onto a useful, well-paying, and interesting job. The prospect is grim for these millions; but it is even worse for those

who have come out of prison or who will be coming out of prison in the years ahead.

For most of what is bad in prison the blame should be placed directly on the prison establishment. But not entirely: for the lamentable fact is that most prisoners are poorly equipped to hold jobs through inferior job training and education. It is unreasonable to expect that prisons with an annual per capita budget of under thirty cents for both academic and vocational education can conceivably do as much or more than public schools whose per capita budget in 1970 was just over eighteen hundred dollars. That so much of prison life involves forced idleness is only partly due to the establishment's need to degrade its captive population; without major reforms outside of prison nothing done in prison is likely to make much difference anyhow. In fact, conditions in prison are likely to get worse.

Although people with prison records have much higher rates of unemployment than any other group in America, there are probably four times as many Americans with serious job problems who have never been in prison. A national policy that would give priority in jobs to offenders over those who have never committed a serious offense would make no sense, even with the certain knowledge that jobs for offenders would make a big reduction in the number of crimes committed and the number of people returned to prison. Without a change in national manpower policies the underskilled, undereducated, underemployed, and unemployed—both those with and without prison records—are going to have to compete with each other for menial, casual, and poorly paid jobs. Tragically, these two groups who are obliged to compete with each other are next-door neighbors in the nation's slums—one a criminal group, the other its victim. The most frequent victims of the most serious crimes live in the poorest neighborhoods and most desperate slums of America. At a time when unity among America's ethnic minorities has grown in importance as both defense against a racist establishment and as a means for making inroads against that establishment, prospects for even more powerful unity are weakened by the fierce competition among the poor—not over the issue of who shall lead but simply over who shall survive.

Since the riots of the 1960s a unique kind of unity has emerged from the ethnic ghettos that is directed towards the blessings of equal rights—but not equal Constitutional rights; the goal of this new unity is equal rights in underworld activities. From the days of the crooked land schemes carried out by America's founding fathers until the 1950s, America's vast criminal underworld has been dominated by white leaders. Waves of immigration produced sharp competition not only for jobs but for effective control of crime. Members of one ethnic minority replaced members of other groups as kingpins in the criminal world; and as fruits of crime were invested in legitimate enterprises, criminal leadership found it difficult to maintain a closed door to aspiring criminal elements from either new immigrant groups or the oppressed minorities.

The white underworld has traditionally been the most brutal exploiter of minority communities. Gambling, drugs, prostitution, loan-sharking, and theft have been financed by and produced profit for white underworld bosses. These enterprises are rapidly coming under the control of minority criminals and unless the struggle for control of crime is reversed, by the end of the 1970s crime in America will be dominated by black criminals—who by that time will be investing their illegal profits in legitimate businesses much as their white predecessors did.

This same pattern of ethnic succession and competition for the reins of crime is going on in our prisons. Until the promises of equal rights and full civil rights are translated into the realities of jobs, business, and industry for all Americans, minority groups will continue to produce a disproportionately high number of offenders—and most of the profits of crime will remain in the neighborhoods that produce crime. In prison, the struggle for minority control over illegal prison power will have disastrous consequences. Jobs for people with prison records are not going to make much difference in the struggle for control of the underworld. The unprecedented attack on organized crime begun in 1970 by the Nixon administration will make black succession somewhat easier to achieve. Inasmuch as Black Capitalism, vaunted by both Presidents Nixon and Johnson as lofty goals, has produced no new black capitalists and hardly any new major black business enterprises, pressure will remain intense for many blacks to persevere in underworld activity in order to become rich and influential through crime as their predecessors did: the Italians from the early 1930s to the present, the Jews in the decade before, the Irish from the 1880s to the beginning of Jewish ascendancy, and the Anglo-Protestants before them. It is doubtful whether this historical pattern of succession can be altered; but its impact on people's lives, especially on the lives of its victims, can be largely mitigated by making poor and jobless people less vulnerable to criminal predators. This can be done through jobs and income providing the means for exodus from the slums.

A dramatic shift has to take place in America with regard to a fundamental commitment to a policy of full employment. Employment policies have so far been prostituted by cynical "buts": full employment *but* unemployment kept at four per cent; full employment *but* no plan to offset the hardship of a million workers who are put out of work each year through automation; full employment *but* no provision to create jobs for the million youths who enter the labor market each year; full employment *but* allowing employers to continue to discriminate against minorities; full employment *but* keeping people with prison records out of the labor force for long periods of time.

A policy of full employment which assures a decent job tied to tough civil-rights laws that vigorously enforce prohibitions against racial discrimination and provisions that no one shall be barred from a job because of a prison record would make sense. Policies like these would contribute much to solving the reentry problems of offenders, reduce the tensions in prisons, and help immeasurably to reduce the conflict between minority groups.

What's more, such policies would help to make an immediate and big reduction in violent crime. Even with full employment, petty crime will continue and prison reform will not have much impact on it. Department stores will continue to lose 10 per cent of their inventory each year through shoplifting and thefts by their employees. Other kinds of change and reform will have to deal with this problem. Regular, secure, decent jobs would do much, however, to reduce violent crime.

Job Training and Education

Without a major revamping of national manpower policies prisons cannot be expected to accomplish very much in the way of mass preparation of inmates for jobs through training and education. However, apart from the limitations of labor-market mechanisms over which prison officials have little or no control, many worthwhile goals can be pursued to provide valuable help to a large segment of the prison population.

A starting point would be the establishment of public policies that direct prison officials to achieve specific minimum goals each year. Just as employees in offices and factories are expected to fulfill minimum levels of productivity, we should demand that prison personnel deliver on what we expect that prison should accomplish. Each community from which offenders are removed and to which many will eventually return should make up its mind about specific performance goals. Without these, prison personnel will continue to do only what they have been doing for two centuries—maintaining a semblance of order, making men worse criminals. It should be possible, for example, for a community to decide that each year its prisons should train, educate, and provide jobs for a predetermined percentage of inmates. To accomplish such a goal would obviously require cooperation from the community-at-large, employers, unions, and agencies of government. If the goal is met, the community should be able to set even higher goals; if it is not met, it may inquire into the reasons for the failure and to take measures to improve performance. The job security of prison personnel should be related to performance up to standards set by the community: standards we badly need but presently do not have for *any* law-enforcement agencies.

Without precise standards that oblige prison personnel to achieve specific goals, much of the criticism of current prison job-training and education programs tends to be either vague or merely touches on superficial symptoms of deeper problems. For example, there is a midwestern federal prison in which the total vocation-training equipment for its nearly one thousand inmates consists of one electrical motor, manufactured in 1914, used by the army for several years, declared surplus in 1920, awarded to the prison in 1922. There are probably tens of thousands of ex-prisoners who retain a sentimental attachment to that motor.

Beginning in 1969, the U.S. Labor Department spent millions of dollars to set up job-training programs in about thirty state prisons. An evaluation of this effort reported in 1971 that inmates who received special job training did not fare much better after their release from prison than inmates who did nothing in prison or who were assigned to routine prison jobs. The report noted that one important reason for this failure was that the kinds of training programs that were initiated were not based on the kinds of jobs that were available in communities to which prisoners would be released, but on what kinds of equipment were already available in the prisons. Installing modern factory equipment in prisons to train inmates for jobs that are, or will become, available seems like a vast and unnecessary waste of money. It would be much simpler to send prisoners, according to their interests and aptitudes, to nearby factories and offices to learn.

Prison visitors are struck by widespread idleness. Their observations are accurate and prison officials do not deny that they have not been able to overcome idleness. There just isn't enough to do in prison—that is, without returning to the evil practices of mass forced labor. Prisoners and slaves in ancient Egypt built pyramids; prisoners of the Romans built amphitheaters from England to Asia Minor; in more recent times prisoners built ocean-going galleons in which they later manned the oars. Properly organized, America's prisoners could within a year's time build a hospital in each of the nation's nearly 3,000 counties, thousands of schools, hundreds of thousands of homes. These things can and should be done—but without resort to unpaid labor or building things that, like the pyramids are mute reminders of human cruelty and vanity.

In 1970 there were over ten million adults in the United States who had not learned to read and write, or who had as much as an eighth-grade education but were still functionally illiterate—and this in a nation that spent, between 1965 and 1970, more on all forms of education than all the other nations of the world combined. But in spite of America's intense and expensive commitment to education, the benefits of education have not yet reached ten per cent of our adult population.

It should not be surprising, then, that 40 per cent of our prisoner population cannot read or write. Countless stories are told about released offenders who are informed that a job may be waiting at such and such company located at the intersection of two avenues with such and such names and that they can get there by taking a combination of such and such buses. But many of the offenders never get there. They are not able to read street, bus, or office signs and they are, understandably, embarrassed to ask.

Educational opportunities and quality education have not been made available to all our people in any way that could be characterized as consistent with democratic principles. The poor of America receive the leftovers of our phenomenally vast educational product. Education for the poor—adult and child alike—has been an abysmal and tragic failure. When, more than a decade ago, educator James Conant declared in his book *Slums and Suburbs* that the qualitative and quantitative imbalances of our national school apparatus were creating an "explosive situation," most people agreed—but few acted. In most urban schools, the situation has gravely deteriorated in the ten years since Conant issued his dire prediction. The levels of educational achievement in reading are far below those of a generation ago. School violence, in both elementary and high schools, is so rampant that uniformed police, as well as young-looking law-enforcement agents impersonating students, work full-time in thousands of schools to prevent explosions, knifings, shoot-outs, riots, and mayhem.

Educational centers for adult illiterates have fared no better. Several recent research evaluations of state-run, federally financed adult basic education programs around the nation show, without qualification, that these efforts are poorly run and produce little if any benefit for the adult learner in terms of improved ability to read and write. Worse, those who run these programs are not complying with the enabling legislation requiring that basic learning be directed towards those intellectual skills that will help the adult illiterate get a job or improve his job situation. English-speaking adults are being taught the same drivel that is being taught without useful results in the elementary schools. Spanish-speaking adults are able to learn little of value. The situation is paralleled in our prisons only in a more concentrated way. The results are far more deprivational.

For nearly forty years, those who have studied juvenile delinquency have repeatedly pointed out that children who do poorly in reading in their school classes are likely to commit delinquent acts and that a high percentage of youthful delinquents become adult offenders. Schoolchildren, especially poorer ones, who cannot keep up with school work suffer humiliation, boredom, restlessness, and disappointment and these lead to a burden of frustration that is expressed in criminal actions.

According to the 1970 final report of President Nixon's Task Force on Prisoner Rehabilitation, fewer than 5 per cent of the nation's prisoners are involved in any kind of rehabilitation program, and only about 1 per cent is involved in any kind of educational program. Moreover, less than 3 per cent of all prison spending goes for the totality of rehabilitation programs with less than half of one per cent of the total annual prison budget going for education. The total federal expenditure for education of our prisoners in 1970 was just over $1.5 million. This amount averages out to about sixty cents per year per prisoner for all prisoners (2.5 million of them); or, if a more positive way of looking at a dismal picture is wanted, fifteen dollars per inmate was spent for education in 1970 for all long-term inmates who were released from prison in 1970 (100,000 of them).

That we continue to send illiterates to prison and release them, still illiterate, leads to the conclusion that we are courting further violent offenses by our continued inability to respond to a fundamental need and right of all people. During the 1950s, when the prison establishment demanded higher salaries, they contended that they could do a better job and "had to do a better job" because prisons were "schools of crime." The 1960s heard the same demand for more money —not for the education of prisoners, but for higher salaries —and this demand was accompanied by the fear-arousing slogan that "prisons are colleges of crime." On December 6, 1971, President Nixon exhorted prison officialdom to "blaze a trail of prison reform," because, he believed, prisons are "universities of crime."

And in many respects the slogans are accurate enough. Prisons don't teach much more than newer techniques of crime, more daring, and indifference to the consequences of crime. Since so many offenders return, they are, in a sense, rounding out their education in crime through refresher courses and advanced training. This is tragic, since the potential is considerable for transforming major segments of the prison apparatus into educational systems that are truly useful and relevant to the real world.

Inexpensive educational programs could be mounted immediately in nearly every prison across the country. Education programs, though, have to be integrally tied to the community reentry problems that face prisoners: establishing a home, gaining the confidence of neighbors, getting and keeping a job. Education for education's sake is sheer twaddle— a mystique propounded by the powerful leaders in the professional teaching community. It comprises an ideology that is perfectly acceptable for the haves, it is a monstrously self-defeating philosophy for the have-nots. And the most deprived of the have-nots are found in our prisons.

Whether prison guards and probation and parole officers are trained to teach, or professional teachers can be induced to spend time teaching prisoners, or whether a national service corps of teachers is employed to do the job is not an important issue in considering prison reform. Nor is the method used to teach a key issue. The overriding issue for prison reform is that prisons should become centers for community reentry, places where, among other things, people have a right to be educated, not because they are prisoners but because they are Americans and all Americans have this right. A variety of gradual, phased educational efforts should be initiated tied to gradual, phased reentry. And there are no formulas or instant educational miracles for prisoners any more than educational experts have discovered instant education models for all America. It matters little, until there is more certain understanding of the learning process, whether work should be combined with study, precede it, or whether basic education should be prerequisite to all subsequent education and job training. What works best for whom can only be determined after much trial and error and cautious, critical evaluation. What is more important is that massive education and training programs should be initiated promptly and pursued with profound seriousness and awareness of their urgent necessity.

What's To Be Done?

Idleness in prison cannot be corrected by patchwork measures; massive public-works programs are going to be necessary as part of a national manpower policy for all Americans in need of jobs, including inmates and people with prison records. Idleness cannot be remedied by prison education programs unless such programs are related to the needs of the nation. Prisoners should have access to quality education because all Americans should have such access. There is no doubt that enough inmates could be trained during their prison terms to become doctors to decisively end a shortage that the medical profession has described as critical for the past fifty years.

Officials of the federal prison system are mindful of this potential: in 1970, for example, an attempt was made at the federal prison in Springfield, Missouri, to launch a training program for hospital technicians. About one hundred inmates would have been trained for well-paying jobs in a field with virtually guaranteed immediate placement. But the warden and his cadres scuttled this project of training because they felt that there wouldn't be enough inmates around to mop the floors and wash the dishes. So the vicious cycle begins to spin: when the community has no jobs for which prisoners can be trained, prison officialdom can justify idleness; when the community has jobs, officialdom can insist that training for these jobs would disrupt prison operations. Training and education can and should be provided in prison; it will help many offenders to shorten the period of time that it takes most to reestablish themselves in a normal community life. So far as prison reform is concerned the issue boils down to one question—not whether training and education should be provided, but under whose auspices? In many states inmate education is carried out by the state education authority, in others by the welfare agency. In an undetermined number of prisons, a guard may be assigned to teach or a local schoolteacher is hired to spend several evenings a week in the prison conducting classes. Often, a guard in charge of inmate education will simply assign inmates who have had a high-school education or some college to organize and carry out educational programs for other inmates.

Vocational teaching follows the same erratic patterns of responsibility. In many states, job instruction is provided by a state agency concerned with vocational rehabilitation, or a division of the state's labor and employment department; elsewhere, when prison officialdom is responsible, a variety of patterns may be found, including the use of prisoners as instructors. Often, in the name of vocational training, inmates simply provide free labor for a private contractor repairing or building an addition to the prison. There is neither instruction or an opportunity for it. In the name of vocational training, inmates are often assigned to work gangs to mop the floors of state office buildings or mental hospitals, clean police facilities, trim the lawns of public parks, and maintain paupers' cemeteries. Neither prison personnel or prisoners have any expectation that such menial labor will lead to employment, but officialdom reports such activity as "vocational training."

Certain features of the Manpower Development and Training Act and the Omnibus Crime Control (Safe Streets) Act of 1968 have made it possible for prison officials to hire specialized private training companies to carry on education and job-training programs in the prisons. These companies, however, provide only instruction and neither make any claims nor actually assist offenders in applying what they have learned to real postprison situations. Expansion of work-release programs has added still another type of responsibility for job-related training.

In addition to these many different kinds of auspices, there are hundreds of prisons where inmates may in their spare time produce paintings and handicraft items which may be sold in prison visiting areas or through a voluntary agency in a nearby city. But the sale price of the items produced by inmates is determined by their keepers, and the number of items that may be sold in a given period of time is also arbitrarily regulated. None of all these patterns of responsibility add up to very much that is significant in terms of providing useful learning or helping inmates earn money in legitimate ways. The myriad economic activities that are available to most Americans to supplement their income in their spare time is denied prisoners.

Because of the way prison officialdom goes about its tasks it has made very little difference who runs education and job-related programs or even how much is spent to carry them out. Programs costing upwards of $8000 a year per inmate have not been any more successful than similar programs costing less than $500 a year per inmate. Programs run by state education departments have not been any better than similar efforts initiated and carried out by inmates themselves. These factors should not suggest that it is just too difficult to help prisoners; what *is* suggested is that very little can be done to help prisoners, no matter how much is spent, as long as the present prison establishment continues to exercise responsibility for conducting programs. Education, job training, and jobs should be provided for inmates—but not by prison officials or under the auspices of prison departments.

Some Proposals

Five very different kinds of auspices should be tried. Each should be evaluated to determine which one or combination works best. If none of them successfully accomplishes *specific performance goals* established by community policies calling for the scheduled reduction of prison populations and phased return to community usefulness, then none should be continued and new approaches developed and tried. One of the very traditional, arrogant acts by the prison establishment is to permit millions of dollars to be spent on evaluation of prison operations and programs only to throw out the results of research that are critical of the establishment and to continue wasteful programs that are guaranteed to fail.

Among the new auspices for education and training programs to be tried, ideally the best, calls for communities

themselves to assume primary responsibility for direct ac-
countability and control of education, job training, and job
placement for that segment of the local population that has
a difficult time getting and keeping jobs including offenders,
who represent the largest proportion of that segment. It is the
American community which generates the conditions and
opportunities for crime, whose members are victims of crime,
whose working people bear the brunt of the costs of crime;
it is where offenders must inevitably return. The task of
placing restraints on the freedom of offenders must be carried
out in the community and not separated from it. The responsibility for education, training, and jobs belongs to the community and it is here that these activities must go on.

But "community" should not be interpreted to mean the
state or a governmental agency. The power centers of American life in their distrust for community democracy are fond
of pointing out that the community, indeed, controls prisons
through elected legislatures and elected governors who ap-
point boards, commissions, and commissioners. These arrangements have not worked out. They have been costly in
terms of inmate lives snuffed out through official murder, the
personal hardships inmates have suffered through official policies of cruelty, and in terms of the increasing money for staff
salaries and construction.

By community control is meant the direct control by citizen groups, through whatever democratic procedure they
choose, to assume and maintain control over prisons and the
services provided there. National standards and minimum
goals should be established by law so as to assure a minimum
level of uniformity in practice, in the same way the judicial

sentences should state explicity the kinds of things that should be available to assist the community reentry and retention of convicted offenders. If minimum standards are not observed and if minimum services are not provided, then sentences should be waived as an infringement of the rights of the convicted person.

Funds for the operation of community-run prison services or, as they are likely to be called, community education and training centers, would be appropriated by state legislatures. If the states merely appropriated to community groups the more than two billion dollars that are presently being wasted, the immediate savings on prison operations would be great. And in making day-to-day decisions about the operation of community prison services, the voices of prisoners and former prisoners should be heard. If communities were to control prison services in each of the three hundred major labor markets of the United States, the burden for providing education, job training, and jobs would average out to twenty-five offenders per month, based on the figure of about 100,000 adult offenders released from prisons each year. Even if communities succeeded in retaining only half of these offenders the result would be a dramatic reduction both in the amount of crime committed and in the prison population.

What should happen to the nearly 200,000 people who now work in the prison establishment as administrators, guards, parole and probation agents, in a variety of other unproductive jobs? Many are eligible for retirement and should be encouraged to retire. The bulk of the workers in the prison establishment should be provided with opportunities to transfer to other governmental agencies. Others should be dismissed—something that should have been done a long time ago. Without doubt there are some thoughtful, idealistic, and competent people working in prisons who, under drastically different control, would be excellent to have in key positions. These should be given an opportunity to become employed by community groups.

The educational and job-related services and opportunities that community groups would provide would be relevant to the communities themselves, and not to the quirks of prison officialdom and the profit-motivated pleadings of special-interest groups. In many prisons it was recently fashionable for prisoners to take correspondence courses in Shakespeare's plays. Prisoners were not asked whether they needed or wanted Shakespeare, but once prison officialdom made the courses available because an educational company had sold them the idea, inmates enrolled in the courses and no doubt many found the Bard enjoyable. But in many prisons large numbers of inmates speak only Spanish and their desire for courses to teach them English has been thwarted by the establishment. Spanish-speaking inmates in prisons where none of the staff speak the language have a difficult time explaining critical health problems, family needs, or personal difficulties. Some sulk, some commit suicide, some die because serious medical problems cannot be communicated, most become helpless pawns in the power games of the establishment.

A second type of control auspices for prisons and prison services involves transfer of responsibility for the running of prisons to private corporations. Corporations could be created for the express purpose of running prisons and providing services to inmates. Existing industrial companies could set up special divisions for the operation of prisons. In much the same way as units of government announce and subsequently award contracts for the construction of post offices and hospitals or the provision of services, private corporations would submit bids for operating prisons. Private companies, either new ones or existing ones, without the endless delays and the suffocating effects of governmental red tape could construct and manage many different kinds of halfway houses, sheltered workshops, satellite communities to industrial centers, as well as transitional communities. A main purpose of each of these would be to provide the means for gradual, phased reentry into communities freely chosen by offenders when they feel and act strong enough to live with a sense of personal self-worth, maturity, and independence.

Contracts with private companies would be set up to require adherence to specific performance goals in terms of reduced prison population, raised educational levels, crime reduction, legitimate employment, and wage levels. Funds for the operation of these private companies would come from funds presently used for prison operations. The primary incentive for private companies to enter this area would be profit, and such profit would be justified by demonstrated performance in making inmate tax-eaters into taxpayers, helping inmates become full citizens in self-government rather than nurturing in them a hatred for democracy. It should be possible through the creation of publicly owned corporations for a wide range of prison operations and services to begin paying the public dividends instead of taking more taxes away for more of the same system of guaranteed failure. Contract awards with private companies who are successful in restoring offenders to usefulness would be continued; failures would be replaced.

An advantage of privately run prisons over community-run prisons is that the profit incentive of the private companies would act as a constant spur to improved performance. A disadvantage is based on the fact that private companies generally are insensitive to community needs and resist listening to community spokesmen—and any private venture in prison services must maintain close and cooperative relationship with communities.

A third type of auspices would involve the transfer of responsibility for prison services to nonprofit or limited-profit corporations owned and run by inmates and former prisoners. These would be established as cooperatives in which any profit produced is shared equally by all members or invested in enterprises that will accrue to the benefit of inmates during the period of restrained freedom or when they are free of restraint. In the long run, inmate cooperatives would likely produce the best and most enduring results compared to other auspices but in the short run would be chaotic and more costly than present prison operations. Temporary chaos would result from a sharp conflict along racial lines that could only be partially resolved by creating racially and ethnically segregated prisons. Inmate-run prisons could probably work successfully without racial conflict or internecine power struggles, but inmates would have to accept the principle of binding arbitration and the presence of arbitrators to reconcile differences. Cooperatively owned and inmate-run prisons would encourage active participation in democratic decision-making for decisions that have vital interest for inmates; in spite of eruption of conflict that would represent growing-pains of prison democracy, this form of auspices deserves a chance to be tested.

A fourth type of auspices involves the transfer of prison responsibility to community institutions. Some prisons, for example, might serve solely as educational centers, and these should be attached to community colleges, senior colleges, or universities. Dormitories, dining rooms, classrooms, and other student facilities would be used for inmate and regular students. To bring about such a change in auspices and to provide incentives for the educational establishment to support the change, Congress should amend the Higher Education Acts to encourage schools to provide facilities and services for offenders.

Some prisons might call for an intensive emphasis on medical treatment and should be attached to medical schools and hospitals. Under these arrangements, inmates could be treated and trained, at the same time, for jobs in the allied medical fields. Some prisons might serve exclusively as centers for vocational education and specific job training and attached to appropriate public and private community-training organizations. Some prisons might serve exclusively as centers for business, manufacture of goods, and provision of services; they could be attached to related enterprises in the community. Incentives could be provided by Congress and state legislatures to encourage business and industry to add residential facilities to their business sites so as to accommodate offenders and their families. Congress might even contemplate a law that would prohibit the construction of any kind of prison with federal funds *unless* it is built as a part of or satellite to a business, manufacturing facility, hospital, or school. Part of such consideration should be given to a requirement that new residential construction with federal funds should earmark a specific amount of living quarters for offenders and their families.

Finally, another type of auspices would entail the creation of a national semi-governmental agency or corporation to take over and run all prisons and prison services in the nation. A national corporation would be in a position to undertake several major innovations as regards violent offenders. First, it would be able to initiate prompt reforms in all those penal institutions where for some time to come violent offenders should be confined. Minimum decent standards for food, sanitation, recreation, health, and legal services could be introduced to remove inhumanity and oppression as the mainstays of prison operations and the basic cause of prison unrest and revolt. The national agency would be able to create a range of diversified and specialized services and facilities relevant to the needs of inmates and communities in ways that would not be hindered by local jurisdictional boundaries based on geographic factors. Unhampered by civil-service regulations, the national corporation could attract and hold onto qualified personnel to perform routine security services needed to fulfill court orders. It could also attract experts in education, job training, and job placement to solve the tough employment problems of offenders. Such a national agency would be guided by policies set up by Congress and by a board of directors made up of ordinary citizens.

The nationalization of our prisons and the transfer of responsibility for their operation to a public corporation would help balance the many inequities that exist in the present system: probation and parole agencies in some states and cities, none in others; physically attractive minimum-security prisons in some places, decaying hundred-and-fifty-year-old fortresses in others; accessible institutions where families can visit prisoners once or more a week in contrast to remote prisons where visits are possible only once or twice a year. Nationalization and a national corporation would replace the present vicious establishment and help undo most of what is wrong in the ways prisons are presently run: it can reduce the amount of damage that is done to lives and bring the costs of running prisons down, and it may, over time, help reduce crime and the prison population. It is the least desirable alternative, but if better methods for establishing new auspices aren't tried, it may be the last resort.

No matter what is done in the immediate future to eradicate the insane inhumanity of the system there will be many offenders who will remain unchanged. These are our violent offenders and we simply do not know what makes them tick. An important aspect of prison reform requires the creation of specialized centers for the study of their behavior and trying new methods to help them overcome their violence. Self-government, education, and jobs are not going to help these cruel men and women in the immediate future, but study centers would provide the means to keep communities free from them as scholars and technicians develop the resources needed to help them attain maturity in a shorter period of time. Over time, even the most violent offenders become decent citizens, and we do not yet understand how this happens.

The direction that America must pursue has got to be based on policies that will strengthen local communities to be able to gradually eliminate the root causes of crime while improving the resources and opportunities for all citizens including those who have offended.

REENTERING THE COMMUNITY

Over a hundred thousand long-term prisoners are released each year from federal and state prisons. Some return to the communities they were living in before their arrest, others move to different communities. For fifty thousand of them, there is no home to go to. For six out of ten, there is a job, generally a token job, to qualify these men and women for parole.

At least one in ten gets on a bus or train with no particular destination in mind. Depending on state prison policies and how long a person has been in prison, they may leave prison with as little as fifty dollars or as much as three hundred dollars. It doesn't last very long. They drift to the vicinity of bus and railroad depots, to a strip of sleazy hotels and rooming houses. Despair terminal, the skid rows of America, the haven for drunks, perverts, ex-convicts, the dumping ground of society's social outcasts.

Many ex-con drifters move out of skid row before they get into new trouble. They are often prime targets of local police looking for people who will serve as informers in exchange for a bottle of cheap wine or a bag of heroin. They wander. There are occasional day laborer jobs, petty thefts, intermittent welfare payments. Many cities have developed mechanisms to prevent the rooting of permanent skid rows, but there are no mechanisms to assist the habitués in establishing new roots elsewhere. Drifters from state and federal prisons have to compete for space on skid row with short-term offenders revolving in and out of local and county prisons.

Nine out of ten offenders released from federal and state prisons return to the cities where they lived before arrest. For the next five to ten years of their lives they are worse off than the drifters. Not only are there no established mechanisms to help them reenter community life, but community officials are outright hostile to them. Recognized by police, they are preyed upon so that they will either become police hirelings or lead the police to the scenes of their next crimes. Police know the grim fact that there is a high probability that a man released from prison will commit a new and more serious offense. The policeman's interest is not in preventing the crime but in winning brownie points by making an arrest that leads to a successful conviction.

People with prison records can't get legitimate credit from lending companies or banks, although there are abundant opportunities for "street-corner" credit, available through loan sharks who lend money at usurious rates and only to those who are unlikely to default on the loan. An ex-convict does not default on loans since he usually will commit another crime as the means for paying back street-corner credit.

Ex-offenders generally can't buy life insurance or health insurance. Even when jobs are plentiful a criminal record is a barrier; so most of the jobs that are readily available involve the business of more crime. Their only companionship is among those who ask no embarrassing questions, that is, other former prisoners.

A national prison-reform policy that includes a concern for easing the reentry of prisoners into communities should not operate in isolation from policies that make possible the substantial movement of peoples out of stagnating cities. A starting point would be national legislation providing significant incentives to stimulate geographic relocation, especially for city residents with limited opportunities. Such legislation would also create the mechanisms needed to ease the hardships or relocation by providing plans for community entry. These plans would provide both information and opportunities for work and education, for housing and participation in community decision-making, places to go to and people to talk with about personal dilemmas. Provision would also be made for welcoming and offering hospitality to newcomers. Within the framework of such legislation conditions would be established to pave the way for the community reentry of ex-prisoners and convicted persons alike by requiring the criminal courts and prisons to anticipate and initiate reentry activity the moment a person is convicted.

A major reentry plan could probably be accomplished quickly and in the most practical fashion by expanding residential and job opportunities in those thousands of small towns whose economic base is derived from the proximity of major prisons. There is an abundance of unused land in the vicinity of these towns and home-building costs are far lower than in large cities or their suburbs. These towns should provide opportunities for prisoners to live away from prison, initially on a trial basis, to work there and to mingle freely with the townspeople. Federal legislation would provide funds for home construction as well as for the expansion and improvement of public facilities that would be required for a larger population. The prison, as a physical facility would, in practice, rapidly become an educational, work, planning, and community-resource center. Some of the work that is done in prisons by inmates could continue to be performed there but with inmates living nearby; some of the work could more easily be done outside of prison walls.

Prisoners should not be granted privileges and opportunities that are not available to all Americans. By the same token, except for certain limited, well-defined restraints on their freedom, they should be provided with the privileges and opportunities that *are* available.

At present, close to 70 per cent of the prisoners leaving state and federal prisons are released on parole. Most parolees are required to return to the communities where they resided before being sent to prison. The remainder, "flat timers" as they are called by the prison establishment, are those who complete their sentence and are free to go anywhere—free to drift. It is rare that a person scheduled for parole can choose a different community to return to, even though most states have entered into parole compacts which permit state parole authorities to assume jurisdiction for parolees from out-of-state. Even though a change of community might be an offender's most important life opportunity, the parole bureaucracy is reluctant to make a change possible because it will mean more work for parole agents. Beginning in the late 1950s, the nation's 25,000 parole and probation officers have clamored individually and through their professional association—the National Council on Crime and Delinquency, formerly the National Association of Probation and Parole Officers—for higher pay, smaller numbers of offenders to supervise, and for more parole and probation agents. And these demands generally have been met, although not to their full satisfaction. The number of parole and probation agents has been increasing at about 8 per cent each year, salaries have been going up at about 10 per cent each year, and the average number of offenders supervised by an agent, the case load, has gone down from one hundred in 1960 to eighty in 1970.

To test the claims of parole and probation agents, most of whom have college degrees and social-work training, that smaller case loads will lead to better results—that is, less repetition of crime by those who are supervised—a number of costly experiments were carried out. In essence, these studies compared the achievements of parole agents with case loads ranging from five to twenty offenders with those with loads of eighty to one hundred. In study after study, the results showed that the claims of the parole agents were unfounded. Over a three-to-five-year period, seven out of ten parolees who had had the benefits of intensive parole supervision returned to prison for new offenses, the same rate of return of those who were supervised by parole officers with higher case loads. Parole does not achieve better results than prisons, since seven out of ten persons spewed forth by our prisons are back within three to five years.

The claim is advanced by the prison establishment, and especially the parole branch, that more "community-based" programs for the offender are needed. By "community-based" programs the establishment means only more probation and more parole, and more local prisons. The term "community-based" is intended to convey the sense that parole agents attempt to bring about meaningful reentry of the offender with the view that the offender will be able to successfully establish roots and build a useful life. In 1971 the federal government provided nearly $200 million to the states for prison-related programs, almost half this amount going into "community-based" programs: more probation, more parole, more local prisons. And because the community extension of traditional prisons is unsuccessful the claim is made that citizens are hostile; and to overcome this hostility, more parole officers, more money, and smaller case loads are the answer.

Parole employees behave like prison employees and neither can succeed unless parolees and prisoners have opportunities and choices for different kinds of community living. Some of these opportunities and choices should be made available to offenders, inside and outside of prisons, by communities themselves, and not by pistol-toting agents of prison. There are the rare exceptions, the unusual parole agents, like the unusual prison guards, who extend themselves by helping to ease the reentry of offenders and whose concern effectively breaks the crime-repeating cycle. But exceptions aside, neither parole agents or the other agents of "community-based corrections" that make up the larger prison establishment are either receptive to or capable of responding to the community reentry needs of offenders.

Shortly before release, a prisoner begins to wonder what he is going to be faced with upon his return. If he has been away several years he will want to know what changes have taken place in his community. What resources are available to help him make it once he gets back? Are there new kinds of jobs? Are there training programs? What is the housing situation? Has his old neighborhood changed? Is it still there? Are there new laws, rules, and regulations pertaining to people who have been in prison that will affect his adjustment? Is he eligible for some form of financial assistance? Will all the talk about free legal help actually. mean free legal services for the many problems that will hound him the moment he leaves prison? A morass of civil legal problems have grown up like weeds during his absence and only gradual certainty, gradual assurance will permit him to deal with these problems without self-defeating anger or bitterness: his possessions have been stolen or possessed by a landlord or finance company, his children have been placed in public shelters, his wife fled, loan sharks want their pound of flesh, former prison cronies lure him with lucrative propositions, drug pushers seduce with promises of dreams and tranquillity, and his conviction record looms like an impassable barrier to survival.

For all these questions and concerns there are few answers in the prison library. For inexplicable reasons of prison security he does not have access to a telephone to call a local chamber of commerce. Shall he inquire of his keepers whether he has the right to sue anyone who has deprived him illegally of property? Although there is a national computer center that will, in seconds, answer a police department inquiry about his court record and personal habits, there is no national center where he can inquire whether he can find a decent place to live or where to get a decent job on his release. Guards don't have answers or information concerning these problems. They are not required to. The civilian staff of prisons—psychologists, social workers, doctors, nurses, dieticians, maintenance workers—none are expected to have answers. Their job is to maintain a prisoner's fitness for imprisonment, not his fitness to reenter society. If a person is involuntarily removed from his community because of the law there should be laws pertaining to his effective reentry.

Community reentry is an overwhelming challenge; for many, a trauma. Prisons, for as long as we continue to need them, should begin providing opportunities for reentry from the first day a convict is sent there. The first requirement for phased reentry means reproducing actual living conditions, actual situations that must or are likely to be faced on reentry.

Simulation of real life through socio-drama, group therapy, and sensitivity training are sophisticated devices for sophisticated people that encourage them to look at themselves and at situations in novel or more insightful ways. These devices are most helpful to people who take time out from their normal lives and play-act for a few hours so that they can deal more effectively with a specific situation. This kind of play-acting in the prison setting can never approximate reality. When these devices have been used among inmate groups and their results analyzed, every instance has shown that inmates are usually worse off, subsequently committing more serious crimes than those who have not participated in these simulations. Some behavioral scientists have speculated that one of the reasons why these methods often prove destructive is that immediate application of the gained perception is not possible in the structured prison environment. These insights are only of use in the usual social world. Although inmates learn to be better able to express why and when they become angry, they do not learn, from simulations, how to curb their anger.

There is no substitute for real-life situations. Real life means talking to people as equals, behaving among people as equals. It means learning by doing in settings that are natural and not controlled by persons in uniform authorized to compel behavior by arbitrary rule. Real-life situations mean the opportunity to make legal mistakes over and over again so as to learn how to get results in accordance with one's goals; it means daily hope and opportunity, daily challenges to act and shape the world rather than to resist and retreat from it. In the final analysis, this is what life entails in the free community. Prisons cannot teach these things by exhortation, because exhortation without opportunity is only hypocrisy. This is why a national policy of extending the geographic boundaries of the prison to include entire communities is so important. It is the most direct and simplest way of allowing real life conditions to affect and be affected by the thoughts, feelings and actions of offenders.

The initial stage of phased reentry should begin at the time of conviction and sentence and should include provision for participation in community life. But participation, even with minimal restraint on the offender, is likely to flounder and lead to trouble unless opportunities are provided the offender to acquire the tools for meaningful, constructive participation. Education and training are the essential tools. Equally important are assured opportunities to use these vital tools.

As centers for community reentry, prisons should be required to actively advocate on behalf of prisoners those measures that facilitate reentry and the movement of citizens in the free community. In part, this means the broad expansion of community involvements which have been initiated on a rather small scale in recent years: work release, education release, and furloughs for a variety of purposes. Legislation as well as discretionary governmental authority for these desirable avenues of community participation exists in nearly all states.

In some states these laws and legal authority have been used infrequently, in some states not at all. Wisconsin passed the nation's first work-release law in 1913 but didn't begin to apply this law to the state's prisoners until 1962, and then only in dribbles and for very short-term prisoners. Arizona passed a work-release law in 1969 but the legislature appropriated no funds to carry out the law and for all practical purposes there is no opportunity for work release in that state.

New York State passed a work-release law in 1969 but the total number of inmates participating in work release in 1971 amounted to about five hundred men and women out of a total annual prison population of close to sixty thousand prisoners. The legislature gave the prison establishment great discretion in deciding who would receive the work-release privilege; therefore relatively minor offenders were chosen, and mainly those who at the time of entering the work-release program had less than three months to serve out their sentences.

The prison establishment is reluctant to allow more than a token number of inmates to leave the prison walls for any form of legally authorized community involvement. They have little apprehension about what a prisoner might do who violates his trust during work release or some other form of furlough. Their tokenism is a way of maintaining traditional arbitrary control over those who are kept behind the walls so as to be able to manipulate and engineer their behavior. The game is: "If you play ball according to prison rules . . . we may let you take part in work release." This is the same form of treacherous, unproductive manipulation that is tied to probation and parole decisions. This kind of strings-attached, coercive manipulation is unsound in raising children and is demeaning when used with adults. But the ability to manipulate the lives of offenders is the single most important instrument of probation, parole, and prison personnel when making community-release decisions.

When the prison establishment speaks of "treatment," they mean coercive manipulation and the threat of further punishment. Halfway-house programs, pre-parole release facilities, community residential "treatment" centers provide, under the rubric of "treatment" little more than what was offered in prison: insistence on docile compliance with rules and no effort to remedy the gaps in education, training, or social skills to be better equipped to deal with people as equals. Most of the federal government's commitment to state agencies of $13 million in 1970–1971 for "community treatment" of offenders revealed precisely what the establishment means by "community": establishment of new probation or parole departments in states, counties, and localities where these services did not exist, establishment of halfway houses in or on the fringes of sprawling urban slums and ghettos, the design and construction of local jails and detention centers, and considerable spending on the improvement of agency record-keeping systems. "Community treatment" did not mean opportunities for increased reentry or provision of the tools for effective reentry or retention in the community. Under threat or duress "treatment" is a euphemism for deprivation and punishment. The oppression felt by poor people cannot be remedied by this sort of "treatment"; only opportunities and resources leading to growth and independence can lift this burden. Our captive inmates, we have learned, cannot benefit from "treatment," the suffocating weight of captivity can be lightened only by increased freedom, opportunity, and resources to enhance their chances of "making it."

Those Americans who see and emphasize only the risks associated with allowing prisoners to leave prison during the day or week so that they can hold jobs, make and keep friendships, maintain family ties at a level that approximates the normal, should consider the well-established risks of not allowing the expansion of such desirable practices—the high rate of return to prison for more serious crime and the heavy burdens placed on innocent victims, prisoners' families, and communities. We know, with a degree of certainty that comes close to scientific accuracy, that the conventional methods of the prison establishment—inside and outside of prison walls—will, over a five-year period, return seven out of ten offenders to prison. We also know, but with much less certainty and precision, that community opportunities that are generous and meaningful help to reduce the high return rate, help to retain a large number of offenders in active, useful community lives, help them to achieve maturity more rapidly. Prison officialdom must advocate these opportunities —to get them started and to sustain them, even though there will be disappointments. Altogether too often, worthwhile community programs for offenders flicker out because there is no one to keep the fires going, to sustain community interest, to keep demonstrating the many benefits of these programs. It should be the prison establishment's obligation to keep these fires going, to advocate the continuation of worthwhile efforts, to advocate newer and broader opportunities not in the name of "treatment," but on behalf of building communities and strengthening the lives of people who live in them.

An additional important advocacy role for prison officialdom involves pressing for speedy, accelerated improvements in the machinery of the criminal and appellate courts. The archaic, chaotic quality of the courts undoubtedly contribute to crime, there is no doubt about it; although they cannot be blamed for the commission of all serious crime, which on the average increases, according to the FBI, between ten and fifteen per cent each year. No less an authority on the courts of America than the Chief Justice of the Supreme Court has vigorously attacked the breakdown in the operations of American courts in general, and the criminal courts in particular. Endless delays, inadequate, often incompetent legal representation of criminal defendants all add up to a wretched system that provides little justice.

Many Supreme Court decisions, especially during the 1960s, have made it necessary for the sentences of many prisoners to be judicially reviewed. But such review is not automatic, and the legal communities of the states have not rushed in the wake of these decisions to assure that a timely and prompt review takes place. Each year since 1965, legislation has been proposed in the Congress making periodic appellate review of criminal sentences mandatory, and each year the legislation was defeated. Inmates who have the means to retain private legal help to pursue costly appeals are in the minority. The vast majority of offenders need advocates to take up a cause which the Supreme Court has said is a valid one for them. Most criminal sentences should be reviewed intensively and regularly for there is more than a remote possibility that thousands of prisoners are presently serving time illegally. Since the means for such review do not presently exist on a meaningful scale outside of prison, the prison is the place, at least the starting place, for such preliminary review—ultimately for the advocacy of full judicial review. For if the prison establishment wishes to validate prison "treatment," then it ought to start treating inmates with a dose of the rights to which they are entitled as a matter of law.

Much of the friction and tension between inmates and guards is attributable not at all to the mortal fear that captors and captive have of one another, but because the apparatus is not required to do more for inmates than to keep them in captivity. The attitudes of hostility often originate with the terrible inefficiencies of the criminal courts. Because of delays, drunken judges, allegations—widespread allegations— about how judges buy their positions on the bench, the groveling of inexperienced public defenders before the bench, the threats of prosecutors to win the game of plea-bargaining, defendants are treated to a grim carnival run by the maternal symbol of justice who is less than impartial and truly blind. The hardening of the offender's attitudes begins in court.

Improvements in court procedures and personnel will take a long time to effect. But the many gaps left by the courts can and should be filled by the prison system. Prisons are extensions of the courts. Since the courts are the final arbiters of the rights of people, the prisons must exercise the extended responsibility of assuring these rights in the same way that, in principle, the ordinary citizen has easy access to the courts in his community. By enmeshing the prison and community into a larger enterprise it becomes possible, with little delay, to right the wrongs committed by the courts. And for prison establishmentarians who disclaim such responsibility—by saying that, by doing these things, they would soon be righting the wrongs inflicted on offenders by inept teachers, an inadequate job-training and manpower system, by poverty and bad housing—the answer is, Yes, they ought to be doing these things, because prisons are integral parts of communities, and all communities should be doing these things. Most of our prisoners represent the bottom of the barrel of America's poor and deprived minorities and we know how they have been crippled by prejudice and discrimination with less than equal access to law and the courts. Special mechanisms must be made available to equalize opportunities for legal redress for anyone who is denied access to the impartiality of justice—including prisoners.

As centers for community reentry, prisons should be able to play an extremely important part in bringing together into a single cooperative relationship the many elements of collective life that help to distinguish between habitations and communities. Both organized and informal elements of communities and neighborhoods—recreation, cultural expression, opinion-shaping forums, religion; economic aspects of communal life like banks, business, industry, consumer centers; the educational arrangements and legal apparatus—should all be built into the prison framework as part of a larger community enterprise. The health services of communities, so antiquated and lacking in our prisons, should be made part of the larger community reentry system. Modern medical practice emphasizes the great value of relatively free movement in the community for persons recovering from disorders, demonstrating that moving about, relating with others, accelerates cure. But the trend, these days, is for greater isolation of offenders with disabilities. Physicians, psychologists, and teachers increasingly recognize that those who are intellectually deficient benefit by participating in learning and other settings with people their own age provided there are specialized out-patient services available to compensate for deficiencies. But prison officialdom is calling for and getting funds to build new prisons for intellectually deficient inmates, removing them still further from opportunities to experience real-life situations. In addition, small prisons situated in small towns, rather than permitting greater involvement of small numbers of inmates in the life of these towns, are being encouraged to abandon the facilities altogether and transfer inmates to remote regional prisons where there are few, if any, chances for community involvement on the part of ordinary citizens or inmates.

If we abandon, as we should, the notion that a court sentence is punishment and prison is the place where punishment is carried out, the sole justification of a criminal sentence is to help the offender establish viable, rewarding community roots. Where these roots grow deep, that is, where the rewards of community life are ample and where there is community-wide effort to retain its members, few will be driven to leave on their own accord, few will be driven out because of crime.

Cooperative arrangements between community and prison do not exist at present. The prison establishment resists the intrusion of broad-gauge community involvement. When selected community groups are vocal and insist on participating in the challenging task of facilitating prisoner reentry, officialdom yields, but only for limited programs that slowly dissipate and disappear. Programs of women's groups are especially vulnerable. They generally volunteer to teach reading or, with their own materials, run craft and art classes. High school and college groups enter into brief alliances with prisons to teach inmates, but are eventually thwarted by prison schedules and dwindling attendance of inmates whose participation is curtailed because of infractions. Private physicians often volunteer their services but leave in disappointment when they discover appalling equipment, few supplies, and the extensiveness of sickness and physical disability. A few organizations like the Jaycees "adopt" prisons as an organizational commitment for members to take part in on their own time. Some assist inmates in getting jobs, helping in other ways at the same time. For many years the Presbyterian Church of America encouraged its members to volunteer time to write letters to inmates to ease their loneliness, but over time, the effort was abandoned by most members, without explanation.

Occasionally an individual—a priest or businessman or former inmate—will over a period of many years sustain a private, serious commitment to visit prisons, to help an inmate during his sentence and after his release. But because these efforts are unrelated to one another or to the community at large, because they are fragmented, they cannot overcome the torpor and basic resistance of the prison system. They flounder, the individuals lose interest and turn to activities where the results are more visible and can be achieved sooner. Individually, they can achieve little. In concert, they can bring about major prison reform, especially since one of the major reforms possible *is* community involvement.

But there has to be a note of caution: in the wake of a prison riot, the establishment likes nothing better than to create a semblance of community involvement. An appearance of reform is generated because reputable community leaders are seen by the public looking over the havoc while making pronouncements that things are going to change. This happened in South Carolina when in 1969, after some bloody, destructive prison riots, the Jaycees embarked on their most active campaign to visit the state's prisons, enrolling inmates. Other groups joined the visiting program. But the squalor and mediocrity of the state's penitentiary in the capital at Columbia was unaffected: vicious dogs patrolled the prison perimeter, inmates were allowed to bribe guards to leave prison grounds to visit houses of prostitution across the street from the prison, the wives of state legislators continued to have their antique furniture mended by prisoner labor and with state supplies.

When an offender leaves prison he does not automatically reenter the community in the full sense of the word. Physically, of course, he reenters a geographical area, but this is by no stretch of the imagination a move towards involvement and participation in the life of the community. Reentering the social compact implies rights, privileges, responsibilities, and for most offenders, at least for a prolonged period of time after release, living in a sort of involuntary limbo. Neither full outcasts or full members of the social compact, neither do they know what rights have been restored to them nor does anyone tell them. Although obscure law journals, from time to time, deal with the complex legal issues about when and how full rights may be restored, most judges and lawyers, prison officials, inmates, and the ordinary citizens are in the dark about this vital concern.

No two states are alike in respect to restoration of rights after a prison term has been served. At the time of sentence, judges generally do not inform offenders how and when they may regain their rights. At the time of release, prison officials are no more informative. Without community opportunities and relevant resources, a social limbo becomes, like prison, another tangible, separate world, a world of skid rows, migrant labor camps, a murderously competitive and exploitative underworld nurtured by paid informers, corrupt policemen, well-financed organizations of criminal entrepreneurs— a lower depth breeding violence, hatred, and crime.

Reentry of the offender into social limbo is an important contributor to further crime. Present prison policies condone and foster this kind of meaningless reentry. The offender cannot successfully reenter the community until provision is made for the full reentry of all who inhabit social limbo, for *all* Americans who have never been afforded the opportunity for full participation in the social compact.

Reentry does not require that all sources of strain and social instability be eradicated or even dealt with in order to open up some of the main avenues of social participation. It will take a long time for offenders to be able to come to grips with the many problems that disorganize their lives, pressing them into desperate and irrational courses of action: family hostilities and marital difficulties, health and learning problems, lack of job skills, drug abuse, youth, immaturity. The cumulative effects of these strains along with the anger and stigma from prison experiences do not lend themselves to simplistic solutions. Solving even part of these problems should not be a precondition for reentry and social participation.

One of the greatest sources of hypocrisy in the prison world has to do with establishmentarians determining whether offenders, as conditions for parole release, have been able to solve some of their problems. Prison and parole agents ask inmates whether they recognize their personal guilt, have more positive attitudes towards their families, realize that a Dale Carnegie drive to win friends and succeed will surely lead to maturity. And inmates attend prison religious services to show contrition, talk with social workers about their evolving mature judgment, write letters they know prison censors will read, letters filled with expressions of remorse and resolve to lead constructive lives on reentry. It is a mass con-game between inmates and prison personnel—neither believing the other, each trying to outwit the other. Eventually parole decisions are based on factors having little to do with the hypocritical con game.

Some of the personal problems of inmates will never be solved; in time, though, the stress and severity of the problems will lessen, and the lessening will in itself have a beneficial effect. With many opportunities for social participation, the chances will increase for many offenders that they will discover ways to deal with their personal difficulties or that new and challenging relationships and responsibilities will help them become less preoccupied with real or imagined emotional wounds and slights from families, communities, and a society that had rejected them.

Avenues for reentry and social participation should be opened up on a large scale. And these can best be created in local communities, for people are retained in society not by society in the abstract but in tangible, local neighborhoods. Reentry and retention can be effected only by local schools and colleges, training and retraining centers, churches, factories, businesses, housing facilities, and public services.

Barriers to the numerous avenues of social involvement and participation have to be removed. Some of these barriers will require repeal of laws and change of governmental administrative regulations. In most states that require licenses for barbers and cosmeticians, offenders cannot become barbers or cosmeticians. In states that require licenses for establishments that distribute or sell alcoholic beverages, people with prison records cannot obtain jobs whether the jobs involve driving a truck that delivers beer or mowing golf courses at resorts that sell wine and liquor. Businesses that provide jobs requiring the handling of money prohibit the employment of ex-convicts and so do most government agencies—federal, state, and local. Many labor unions, over time, have broken through these barriers by adopting forward-looking practices in behalf of the offender, but many unions—notably those in the construction trades—have been particularly restrictive both in regard to the offender and minority groups as well.

If there was ever a time that valid justifications existed for excluding offenders from social involvement, these reasons have been lost in the tangled web of history. In a nation with critical shortages of doctors, dentists, and hospital employees there can be no justification for any form of exclusion except on the basis of competence. Yet nearly every state prohibits offenders from becoming doctors. Other professions are off limits to offenders like those of real estate salesmen, billiard parlor operators, veterinarians, embalmers, accountants, and insurance adjusters. Although many seek remedy through the law to gain exemption from these restrictive practices, the bureaucratic machinery is so cumbersome, the procedures so lengthy and costly, that even the most highly motivated and potentially best-equipped for many professions abandon their dreams in despair. For many, access to the law and its protections is remote and few are equipped financially and psychologically to take on a formidable establishment, especially when the American public looks on offenders as a population characterized by low motivation, poor previous achievements, and as basically irredeemable.

A major barrier to reentry and retention is the requirement of most community institutions—educational, employment, even recreational—that an applicant for participation has to indicate his arrest and conviction record. This is the case whether the agency provides jobs or furnishes apartments in a public housing project. These restrictions are intolerable especially during the first few years after release from prison. There should be no requirement for indicating arrest and conviction record for any form of community participation. Criminal proceedings are a matter of public record as far as adults are concerned. Officials of community organizations should be required to assume the burden of determining whether a person has a criminal record and to use such information merely as a guide to prevent stresses from arising that would jeopardize the equal participation of the offender as well as the safety and sense of security of other participants. Such information should not serve as a basis for restraint, restriction, or exclusion. For an offender to be required to indicate a past record of arrest and conviction is tantamount to a subtle but pernicious form of self-incrimination—an action prohibited by the Bill of Rights.

The attitude of the American public towards the offender and the attitude of public officials who speak and act in the name of the public should be changed only in the face of tangible proof that prison reform is able to produce effective results. The harm done to the community by many offenders is too grievous to expect many quick changes. But effective results can be produced quickly with far less spending and with major benefits not only to the offender but to the public as well.

An important element in the reentry process will require the phasing of involvement and participation.

In some communities, prison reform measures will require formal and detailed phasing schedules and plans as well as formal proof that far more protection at far less cost will be generated by reform than by continued restrictive, exclusionary and discriminatory practices. In some communities phasing of reentry will require little more than a visible demonstration that with minimum restraint on his freedom and with maximum opportunity to exercise all the rights of a citizen, the offender will effectively and constructively bridge the gap between conviction and release, between immaturity and maturity, between hostility and communication in far less time than the five to ten years that it presently takes for most ex-prisoners to "make it" after release from prison.

XI
TRANSITIONAL COMMUNITIES —A PATTERN FOR REALITY

An Alternative

SOCIAL CONTRADICTIONS AND
UNREST

For the great majority of her people, America has been bountiful. This does not mean that we should forget the many people, past and present, for whom the American experience has been a devastating nightmare. Open recognition of all forms of inhumanity, resolution to eliminate it at its roots, and commitment to creating a more just society are ways to insure that the bounty of America will be available to all.

The end of World War II ushered in an era of American life in which the contradictory and oppressive sides of that life were laid bare: McCarthyism, militarism, imperialism, racism, consumer exploitation, stifling of lawful dissent, big-brotherism, corrupt and irresponsible government, rigid institutions, violence, irrelevance. A national mood developed that insisted on exposing festering sores in the body of society. There has been no abatement in the exposure of the sordid evils of the American experience. There appears to be no end of inequities.

Some Americans have fled or sought retreat, to tend their gardens. Many agree that, indeed, there are problems, but contend that they are neither so destructive or widespread as to require immediate, fundamental changes. Some cling to the illusion that long-standing injustices can be swept under a carpet by means of repression under a banner of law and order. Still others recognize and accept the enormity of our problems and are resolved to do something about them. Strident cries of "America—Love it or leave it!" are met with shouts of "Power to the people."

The need for change is great. The pace of change is slow, but while the problems and the searing tragedies they produce persist, America is not a sick society. There is no cancer gnawing away at her innards. Such talk reflects either the political agenda of discontents who say that nothing can change unless everything changes or that of messianic politicians who claim that only they can bring about needed change. Progress in America has never come about by changing everything—or by relying on elected leaders. It is the people themselves who change things, given the resources and opportunities. The inadequacies and injustices of America are not going to be rectified by diagnosis, political cant, or threat of dire upheavals. The tools for change are available and change will come about on an ever-increasing scale if the victims of oppression make use of these tools. They are peaceful and lawful tools and the difference between a sick and a

healthy society is not the lack of problems but the availability
of tools to correct the problems.

URBAN ILLS

An especially corrosive problem in America has come about
through the unplanned, unregulated growth of population
that has crowded into cities and their immediate suburbs.
Except for the affluent or near-affluent, no cities anywhere in
the world were ever easy places to live in. Problems of urban
transportation, work, pollution, public services, crime, sickness, responsive local government, quality education, persistent prejudice, and discrimination have been and continue to
be unmanageable. It is very doubtful that given the magnitude of the problems and the continued population growth
in the cities and suburbs that cities will be substantially better
off a generation from now.

Many people born in cities, especially if they are born poor
or into modest economic circumstances, have little to look
forward to as they imbibe the potions of the American
Dream: hard work, keen motivation to succeed, competitive-
ness. The public promise that more education and cooperation with the system are going to provide a more ample share
of the good life has been an empty promise. Beguiled by the
promise, tens of thousands of Negro youngsters completed
high school and even college and find that they are still
without jobs, still live in the squalor of the ghettos. Education
and working within the system are not providing benefits
commensurate with the increasingly grinding effort required.
Even with a trebled rate of residential construction, children

living in slums today will be living in those shoddy places a decade from now. And not even the most optimistic economist holds out much hope that with a greatly expanded economy there will be enough jobs available in the nation's cities for those who are presently unemployed, those whose jobs will be eliminated by automation, and for the million youths who enter the labor market each year.

Even the end of the debilitating war in southeast Asia and the potential return of billions of dollars to the domestic economy will not, in the lifetime of most people living today, result in a significant and more just redistribution of the nation's wealth for our ten million very poor families, most of whom live in cities. For the poor, cities are anathema, a persistent yoke on the enjoyment of fundamental rights: the right to a decent home, to an honorable job with decent wages, a secure and dignified family life from birth to death, and ample field for exercising citizenship.

THE CITY AND CRIME

Crime in America is intricately woven with the complexities and problems of city life. Although 75 per cent of the nation's population live in cities, over 90 per cent of the nation's crime is produced in cities. Much crime in America is violent because city life is inherently violent. Most of our criminals are city people whose resources and opportunities for adjusting to the demands of city life are essentially illegal. They are ill-suited, at least for a major portion of their lifetime, to the erratic, conflicting, and irrationally competitive demands of city life.

Worse, they are ill-equipped to respond successfully to urban demands without running afoul of the law. People who are released from prison and reenter city neighborhoods are destined, especially those of them who are young, to repeat their crimes and with greater violence, and for no other reason than no prison, no matter how near or far from the city's central core, can improve a person's skills to deal with increasingly complex demands of city life. Only real community living can do this.

GETTING AWAY FROM IT ALL

City dwellers who are poor, undereducated, underskilled, powerless, and without much hope for the future do not have the resources and opportunities for more than stark survival in the city. For them, the city is a trap of despair. And because the situation is not going to improve markedly no matter how many changes are introduced in the near future, exodus from the cities should be pursued as a goal of high national priority. Urban exodus should be an alternative not only for poor people and prisoners, but for all Americans who find that city life offers less and less variety, convenience, and security but demands more arduous and costly effort.

Exodus from the city should not imply permanent resettlement. Permanent settlement, anywhere, should be a matter of voluntary choice, provided it is a choice among comparable alternatives. Choice is a basic ingredient of life that is in the shortest supply in prison. The void exists because the prison establishment cannot exist where people who, in spite of ill-defined legal restraints, are essentially free. To be free means to exercise choice among realistic alternatives. The void exists also because prison routine is not geared to improve a prisoner's ability to adjust to live anywhere except in prison. If prison reform could have but a single goal, it should be the creation of real communities without walls as an alternative to the inescapable traps that most cities are for most prisoners.

TO WORK OUT A NEW LIFE

New communities could become but need not be established as permanent settlements. They ought to serve primarily as transitional communities—transitional for prisoners who need time to learn new and improved skills for dealing competently with the demands of modern conditions and who, subsequently, may choose to return to their former city neighborhoods or to an entirely different location. Prisoners might elect at the end of a court-established period of restraint upon their freedom to remain and permanently settle in a transitional community.

Many different kinds of transitional communities are possible and should be developed. All should be established with a view towards providing alternatives to cities for poor people, prisoners, and others who seek an opportunity for a new style of living.

New settlements and transitional communities are not really new ideas. They represent an updated version of what was done, successfully, in America during the period of colonization in the 1700s when thousands of prisoners from English and European prisons gained freedom by emigrating to the New World. Some of America's oldest and most illustrious families trace their ancestry back to these first criminal settlers, whose emigration represented liberation from the putrifying slums and prisons of London, Paris, Amsterdam, Madrid, and other cities. Australia was settled in much the same way. Although emigration of prisoners was sometimes voluntary, it was, more frequently, obligatory. A system of brutal coercion required servitude under indenture-contract arrangements. This represented a small improvement over life in the squalid city prisons. But at the end of the indenture period, carried out in small communities, there was opportunity: land, work, citizenship. Coercive indenture contracts for prisoners are convenient devices for the state, and forms of indenture are still practiced in places like the Soviet Union which has vast, remote areas where labor can be exploited to build new settlements. Transitional communities, like any other form of communal life, cannot long thrive under conditions of coercion. Participation in transitional communities should be voluntary, on the part of the citizens who live and work there, and on the part of prisoners who will eventually become full citizens without any special restraint on their freedom that is not applied to all citizens.

IS IDLENESS REALLY A SIN?

Some will say: what about the prisoners who don't want to work? What about them? The answer is that no one, except in times of the gravest national crisis, should be obliged to work. Mandatory labor, as two hundred years of our prison experience with forced, brutalizing work has shown, leaves us only a heritage of roads, with little additional benefit to the American people or the prison slaves who were bludgeoned into submission to build them. People who don't want to work should be allowed not to. Accepting the idea that prisoners should be free to chose not to work should not serve as a justification for any further restraint on their freedom or for punishment. These inmates should not be denied either creature comforts available to all prisoners nor should they be deprived of other provisions for life that are required by fundamental humanitarian concern for their fellow men. They would not be paid wages and they would not have those many opportunities for growth and maturity that derive from paid work.

Efforts should be made to develop the kinds of incentives that will spark the motivation of those who don't want to work or don't want to further their education or acquire job skills. They should neither be ignored nor looked down on for their refusal to work. They are still at odds with society and its basic requirement; cooperative endeavor for the common good. The fact that this awareness does not move them to appropriate activity means that collectively we have not made either the social good or the social life sufficiently appealing to them to involve them in our common destiny.

NEEDED — REAL WORK

Although hundreds of millions of people the world over work a good part of their lives and work voluntarily, many loathe what they do and reluctantly accept the unhappy conclusion that a major portion of their lives is going down the drain with few joys or accomplishments. This is, sadly, particularly the case in industrialized nations. America is slowly coming to the realization that productivity does not suffer, either quantitatively or qualitatively, from shorter working hours. For many, shorter working hours means liberation from drudgery. Indeed, early retirement for millions of Americans, even with modest pensions or reliance on social security benefits, has not meant inactivity. A 1969 study conducted by the Labor Department showed that retired persons in ever-increasing numbers were devoting a major portion of their retirement to voluntary activities in much-needed community services.

Societies, generally, have failed to provide a wide enough range of opportunities for people to work at what they can best do and what they like best to do. It appears likely, within the next decade, that a working person will be paid a full day's wages but spend only half the time in the conventional office or factory setting and the remainder of the time in some form of community service that corresponds to his abilities and interests. In a more rational and better-ordered society work for everybody will be a source of pleasure and fulfillment rather than necessary monotony.

As American society becomes more affluent, the brute necessity for work diminishes, and we must permit those who choose not to work to abstain until they find their right avenue for expression through productive employment. It is because the right and privilege not to work is becoming increasingly available to all Americans that they should not be denied to our prisoners.

The Prison Town as Transitional Community

Probably the simplest, quickest, and most practical way of establishing a transitional community would be to convert some prisons into factories, schools, hospitals, and meeting places while creating housing, shops, and other community facilities in the vicinity of these prisons. Many families of inmates would probably choose to relocate there to begin to mend the threads of their frayed and precarious lives. States that require educational facilities in areas where there are children of mandatory school age would have to make educational services available to the school-age children of prisoners. Local units of government would be obliged to set up a framework for local self-government for the new inhabitants. Mandatory public services on the state, county, and township levels would, by law, have to be provided: water, sewage, protective services, recreation. In our prisons today, most prisoners have little to care about, little to look forward to, little to cherish in their immediate environment. Only the desire to stay alive, to survive, is what keeps them going from day to day. By converting a prison into a transitional community the prison will be able to fulfill a major traditional goal —one it has never achieved: provision of the tools, resources, and opportunities people need to tap the limits of their abilities.

NEW LIFE FOR THE TOWN

To a considerable extent the thousands of small towns
where prisons are located are one-industry towns. Prisons are
the primary economic base for the townspeople, most of
whom are employed in the prisons or who get a livelihood
from providing direct and indirect services to the prison.
These are essentially self-sufficient communities but economically marginal since the prison economy, at present, has little
or no leavening for growth.

Merging the prison with these communities, permitting
inmates to live outside the walls, and encouraging the expansion of industrial activity would provide inmates with many
incentives that do not presently exist for developing a stable
and mature interest in their work and social relationships.
The same incentives would act as leavening for modernization and economic growth in the prison towns.

Some big prisons, like the Washington State Penitentiary
in Walla Walla, are slowly moving in this direction. Following prison disturbances in Walla Walla in 1970 and the threat
of riots, a few prison officials began to encourage guards to
take inmates home to dinner with them, to take part in
limited fashion in the social life of the prison towns, to allow
inmates to wear civilian dress outside the prison so that the
stigma of imprisonment did not have to show too flamboy-
antly. Washington state AFL-CIO members undertook a
vocational-training program for inmates and are making
efforts in placing graduates into jobs.

Labor-union officers in Minnesota in 1970 began the same
kind of involvement with prison staff and inmates at the

Stillwater Penitentiary. Beginning in 1969 in four industrial cities, the AFL-CIO assigned union officers as "buddies" to inmates, to help them from shortly before to months after release from prison in adjusting to the demands of communities. The National Urban Coalition in 1969 similarly began to encourage its local affiliates to try to create bridges of relationship between prison and community through the intermediary of concerned citizens. In the same year, a federation of Jewish Community organizations in Richmond, Virginia began to take similar steps.

These are sporadic but promising beginnings and they are taking place without an organized national prison reform movement. These reform initiatives are taking place without political or moral polemics about what should be done or why, without a rash of new laws and procedures that become hopelessly entangled in the murky depths of legislative and administrative bureaucracies. These hopeful developments are taking place because the public in its traditional pragmatism has come to recognize that there are better ways of protecting the community from convicted offenders than by locking them up and hoping for the best. A better way is to do what Americans have been doing for a long time, that is, accepting offenders back into communities gradually and with growing trust. There are no laws that require that this approach should take place and no coercion to back up these traditional practices.

More communities, in time, should and will increase their relationships with prisoners outside of the walls and will, also, go the next step to merge the prisons with their communities in the same way that thousands of colleges in small towns are completely interwoven with the towns. This trend is becoming even more pronounced as faculties and students spend more of their time outside of libraries and classrooms, spending proportionately more time among local townspeople, applying knowledge to solving local problems and improving the quality of life for the entire community.

Although thousands of towns rely on prisons for their economic survival, very little of the industrial capability or manpower inside the prisons has any relevance for the immediate and often substantial problems of the towns. Problems like modern sewerage, improved water facilities, flood and pollution control, construction of needed health facilities, are beyond the means of the townspeople. As a result, many prisons are surrounded by towns that have been in continual state of decline, physically and economically. Towns in decline find it difficult to hold onto their youth who move to where opportunities for a fuller life are more abundant and attractive. New ideas for civic improvement, new blood to invigorate old communities, are lacking. As older prison guards retire or die, the states have difficulty recruiting new guards to replace them, especially people from America's black and other minorities who have, because of prejudice, been kept away from America's small, all-white communities. Close to ninety per cent of America's black population live in cities. The majority of inmates in our prisons are black, and the inability to attract black staff to small towns exacerbates an already tense racial situation in most prisons.

In 1971, New York tried to remedy the racial imbalance of staff at Attica by bussing newly recruited minority personnel from Buffalo and Rochester, a distance of thirty to forty miles, to work within the walls of the prison, where only fifteen per cent of the inmates are white, in a small town in which less than one per cent of the population is black. Bussing has raised many complex, often ugly problems when it tries to deal with school desegregation. Bussing of prison guards will raise many new and even more abrasive problems. And the answers will only be temporary.

The underlying problem of these small, one-industry towns is that they are economically dependent on their prisons. Shutting these prisons would be a deathblow to these towns. But merging prison with town would provide for an immediate fusion of new ideas, new blood, new and exciting opportunities through a transformation of prison towns into transitional communities.

Prison manpower and the industrial capabilities of prisons could be applied to the creation, testing, and installation or construction of many needed facilities to respond to the long-neglected problems of the towns. These work activities are encouraged by state laws and increasingly are being supported by federal government grants-in-aid and contracts for such improvements as sewage treatment, watershed development, pollution control, physical facilities for the aged and handicapped, neighborhood rehabilitation, and reforestation. New laws are not needed to permit prisoners to work on these activities, and the communities would derive much benefit. Many houses and farms in these one-industry prison towns have been empty for years and have begun to rot. They could be restored, leased or purchased by inmates and their families, providing a new source of local public revenue. Local schools and small factories that have had to close down because there weren't enough students or workers around could be filled up again, providing all the townspeople, including prisoner residents, with new opportunities for education and work. Small theaters and movie houses which now operate only one or two days a week because there aren't enough people to buy tickets could be restored, thereby providing new cultural and entertainment resources. And with inmates paying taxes because they would be paid scale wages, the tax burden on local residents would be either lightened or the new revenue could be used for expanding local services.

Transitional Communities Away from the Prisons

Transitional communities should be circumspectly considered for the inner cities of major metropolitan areas. Some transitional communities are already in existence in inner cities. Located in ghettos and marginal areas of downtown, halfway houses have been established; some long-vacant buildings have been rehabilitated to provide living quarters to parolees and probationers and temporary residence to convicts as they leave prison and search for living quarters. These kinds of arrangements are the least desirable and delay rather than accelerate opportunities for learning new skills for social living especially in an urban setting. But there are prisoners who, for some time, yearn for their old neighborhoods and the anonymity of the big city. Many prisoners need the possibility for renewing old contacts and family ties. Some of these ties are very weak and were the cause of past troubles. Logically, they should be the ones most to avoid. But as there is no acceptable logic in the criminal's mind, and no sensible logic acquired in prison, return to the seedy, grinding misery of inner-city neighborhoods is an inevitability, however illogical.

Many other pocket-size transitional communities can be established in or near large cities. Some can be created by imaginative use of air space over existing factories and office buildings, providing living arrangements for prisoners and access to jobs. Some can be attached to colleges and universities. But new amendments to existing laws would have to provide increased money incentives to encourage business and educational institutions to take on an additional responsibility.

IN THE DESERTS

There is less need for building halfway houses in the slums and nearby than for developing more attractive alternatives far away from the city. Transitional communities, away from big cities, are just such alternatives.

The deserts of America offer intriguing and challenging opportunities for the creation of transitional communities. Once forbidding, hostile and desolate, inhospitable and barren, many desert communities are now blossoming. Affluence has created among many Americans the need and desire for a second home. Land and community developers have responded to this need and its potential for profit by building a dazzling variety of attractive vacation communities. Mechanized, semi-automated methods for installing water-supply systems, cheap power, and transportation permit both universal air-conditioning and ease of travel. There is an abundance of land in the desert, and before it is entirely transformed into havens of relaxation and retirement for the rich, efforts should be made to create attractive centers of community life for the poor, serving at the same time as transitional communities for prisoners. For the immediate future, most of the economic life of desert transitional communities would have to depend on the governent as the principal employer. But this is no different from what many people have already begun to accept for the millions of persistently unemployed people in the nation—that is, where the private sector cannot grow fast enough to provide jobs, the government must become the employer of last resort.

IN APPALACHIA

Transitional communities could be established with great ease and considerable benefit in the hundreds of towns of America that have been abandoned over the past twenty years. Many of these towns are to be found in the region of economic and social devastation that has come to be referred to as Appalachia.

Stretching a thousand miles from north-central New York to the highlands of Tennessee, Appalachia is a region of played-out coal mines. It was once a region of flourishing but not prosperous communities. It is filled with abandoned school buildings, municipal centers, offices, and shops. Factories, fire stations, and movie houses are boarded up. Parks and gardens have gone to weed. Trees, vines, and plants have begun to erode the foundations of thousands of homes whose inhabitants have fled the region. Macadam roads are splitting. There is an air of desolation, neglect and despair.

Some people have remained in the hollows of Appalachia and in the lonely towns. A few elderly people cling tenaciously to land that has been owned by their families for generations. They eke out a living on a small pension or social security. Many hill people living in tar-paper shanties receive modest welfare payments; they pay five dollars a month rent and drink polluted surface water as it seeps from abandoned mines. There are some children whose parents travel fifty to a hundred miles a day to work in distant factories. Even some of the local prisons have been shut down and prisoners transferred elsewhere.

Here are abandoned but complete towns ready to receive people who could resurrect community life. Here is a prime opportunity for many transitional communities, places where prisoners may volunteer to serve out the remainder of their sentences while learning, relearning, and sharpening their ability to come to grips with the demands of social life, and in a setting offering opportunities to mature and prosper with minimum restraints on their freedom. No new laws are needed to bring about such transitional communities in the ghost towns of Appalachia. Laws already provide for parole or pre-parole release, and in many states prisoners may be sentenced by the courts to reside in communities that are mutually agreed on by the convicted person and the court. In states like Vermont, once the court passes sentence the state's prison commissioner may decide in cooperation with the prisoner to which community he will be sent to serve his sentence. Furlough and work-release laws would also permit the repopulation of ghost towns and the rebuilding of local economies, repairing the social fabric of small towns, providing, at the same time, opportunities for the rebuilding of damaged lives.

No new laws are required for re-creating a viable economic base for Appalachian transitional communities. State and federal laws that regulate the kinds of things that may be produced in prisons permit the letting of many different kinds of government contracts, federal and state, for the production of goods to be used for government purposes. Applying these laws would make possible the creation of a wide range of factory and business activities carried on along modern lines, enterprises that would be profitable and would produce goods for the benefit of all Americans.

ECONOMIC REBIRTH

Prisons now operate, under government contracts, a variety of data processing and computer services. These could be relocated in the empty office buildings of Appalachia. Prisons now operate factories that produce tractors, farm machinery, paints, paintbrushes, electronic equipment, railroad equipment, hospital garments, airplane parts, books, shoes, textiles. These could be relocated in Appalachian ghost towns to reawaken and use once again stilled, empty factories and workplaces.

With their earnings, prisoners could rent or buy apartments and homes that are now empty and decaying. The lights would go on again in these towns. It is probable that the families of inmates who volunteer to relocate in these transitional communities would also want to establish new lives there, and Appalachian schools would open up again. It is probable that businessmen and craftsmen who abandoned their towns when the mines shut down would return to work and to share a community life with the prisoners whose efforts facilitate the rebirth of a local economy.

REAL SELF-GOVERNMENT

Instead of the mockery of self-government that the prison establishment refers to as inmate councils, councils that produce little more than cynicism toward government and democracy, councils that represent "flies governing the flypaper," inmates in a transitional community would be able to participate fully in the affairs of local government including election to local office. Such election would not contravene state laws that presently and stupidly bar people with prison records from holding public office, since the communities are in fact prison communities but without walls. There are no laws that prohibit or impair this form of public officeholding or this form of self-government. Self-governing transitional communities would eventually lead to the abolition of all laws that place unreasonable restrictions on the freedom of people who have been convicted of crimes.

Would crime and delinquency occur in transitional communities? Certainly—but on a level of far less frequency and severity than presently occur in prisons which breed criminality and violence. But transitional communities would eliminate many of the known root causes of crime and delinquency by preventing a crowded physical environment, facilitating

home ownership, providing stable and meaningful employment, fostering active involvement in deciding the day-to-day
issues of a community, offering a sense of growth and genuine
opportunities to build anew on the foundations of social life
that had been criminally exploited by the rapacious mine
owners of a previous generation.

Many young people unfettered by a criminal record—who
presently flee big cities because they are too burdened by
insoluble problems or because cities offer little opportunity
for the play of the imagination in trying novel solutions to
social dilemmas—would be attracted to the transitional communities. There would be fresh outlets for their idealism and
broad opportunities to test new ideas. New styles of life could
unfold in an environment that contains enough physical reminders of traditional values to be of general appeal to most
people—including many poor people who now inhabit the
nation's slums and live with little hope that anyone is going
to make the slums more habitable.

Enforcement of the criminal laws is much less a problem
for America than fuller and more energetic application of
laws that enlarge opportunities and enhance personal and
social rights and obligations, provide incentives for achievements and the peaceful pursuit of material well-being. The
now empty courthouses and police stations of Appalachia
would also have to be used again, but this time with a special
slant on life: not to impose one unworkable and demanding
restraint after another, but to make laws enlarge the human
vision, to expand human freedom.